Starting a Small Business in Connecticut

John S. Purtill, Jr., CPA
Managing Editor

Community Accounting Aid and Services, Inc.

Connecticut Small Business Development Center

ISBN 0-963930-90-7

This material is based on work supported by the United States Small Business Administration under cooperative Agreement Number 4-7770-0007-13. Any opinions, findings, conclusions or recommendations expressed in this publications are those of the authors and do not necessarily reflect the views of the United States Small Business Administration.

This publication is designed to provide practical and useful guidance about the subject matter covered. In publishing this book, neither the authors, the editor nor the publisher are giving legal, accounting or other professional service. They cannot and will not assure that your business will be successful as a result of implementing any advice contained herein. For legal or accounting advice or other expert advice, the reader should consult with a qualified professional.

EDITORIAL STAFF

Managing Editor

John S. Purtill, Jr., CPA   Purtill & Company, Cheshire

Contributing Authors

Steven K. Carter, CPA	Carter, Small + Hayes, PC, New Haven
A. Donald Cooper, CPA	Benevides, Wiseman & Cooper, Ltd.,New London
Sheila K. Garvy, CPA	Purtill & Company, Cheshire
Lester Killen, MBA	CSBDC, West Hartford
Lorraine A. Martin, CPA	Purtill & Company, Cheshire
John J. Palmeri, JD, CPA	Palmeri & Rock, PC, Cheshire
J. Michael Purcell, CPA	Kostin Rufkess & Co, West Hartford
John A. Quebman, BS, BA	InterPay, Inc., Cheshire
Michael E. Regan, CPA	KPMG Peat Marwick, Hartford
Anthony J. Switajewski, CPA	Ernst & Young, Hartford
David Baker, MBA, EA	Shawmut Bank Connecticut, Hartford

Editorial Advisors

Charles J. Frago, CPA	KPMG Peat Marwick, Hartford
John M. Horak, JD	Reid & Reige, PC, Hartford
Edmund S. Kindelan, CPA	Kostin Rufkess & Co, West Hartford
Susan R. Kozera, CPA	Blum Shapiro & Company, Farmington
John M. Lutz, CPA	Arthur Andersen, Hartford
Michael S. Malesta, JD	Kaman Corporation, Bloomfield
Sandra W. Pierog, CPA	Coopers & Lybrand, Hartford
Fredrick L. Robertson, CPA	KPMG Peat Marwick, Hartford
Paul B. Sonoski, JD	Reid & Reige, PC, Hartford
John O. Tannenbaum, JD	Robinson & Cole, Hartford
Ivy F. Zito, CPA	Ivy F. Zito, CPA, Marlboro

ABOUT OUR AUTHORS

Without the efforts and knowhow of our authors, this book would not exist, and we would be without the resources needed to help small business owners. We're proud of them and would like you to know a little more about them.

John S. Purtill, Jr., CPA is Managing Partner and a management specialist with Purtill & Company, Cheshire, which he founded in 1983. His experience includes financial and general management assignments in ABB Combustion Engineering and UNIROYAL. His firm provides services to small businesses including business and tax planning, accounting and business systems. He is author of several education courses sold to CPAs throughout the United States.

David E. Baker, MBA, EA is a Vice President at Shawmut Bank in Hartford. He is an adjunct faculty instructor at the UCONN MBA school and St. Joseph College teaching marketing, management and accounting. He is an instructor for the IRS small business workshop.

Steven K. Carter, CPA is a Partner in Carter, Small & Hayes, PC, New Haven. He has a comprehensive background in not-for-profit organizations and closely-held businesses.

A. Donald Cooper, CPA, is a Partner in Benevides, Wiseman & Cooper, Ltd., New London. Mr. Cooper directs the firm's Management Advisory Services Department, which offers planning and consulting services to small businesses in addition to traditional accounting and tax services.

Sheila K. Garvy, CPA is a Partner in the Cheshire firm of Purtill & Company. She assists small businesses with start-up, tax strategy, and computer software packages.

Lester Killen, MBA is a Business Counsellor with the Connecticut Small Business Development Center, West Hartford Office. Mr. Killen teaches business planning and small business management in adult education programs, community colleges and Chambers of Commerce sponsored seminars.

Lorraine A. Martin, CPA is a Partner in the Cheshire firm of Purtill & Company. She assists small businesses with taxes, accounting and business planning.

John J. Palmeri, JD, CPA is a Partner in Palmeri & Rock, PC, Attorneys at Law, in Cheshire.

J. Michael Purcell, CPA is a Partner in the regional CPA firm of Kostin, Ruffkess & Company, CPAs in West Hartford. He has been in public accounting practice since 1971, advising small businesses on financial, tax and management matters.

Jack Quebman, BS, BA, is President of InterPay Automatic Payroll Service in Cheshire. He has been processing payrolls for small and medium sized companies for over seventeen years.

Michael E. Regan, CPA, is a Senior Manager in the tax department of KPMG Peat Marwick in Hartford. He has had diverse experience with many financial institutions, broker-dealers and closely-held corporations.

Anthony J. Switajewski, CPA, is a Senior Manager in the tax department of Ernst & Young in Hartford. Mr. Switajewski specializes in tax planning for individuals and small to medium size businesses.

MESSAGE FROM THE GOVERNOR

LOWELL P. WEICKER JR.
GOVERNOR

STATE OF CONNECTICUT
EXECUTIVE CHAMBERS
HARTFORD, CONNECTICUT
06106

Throughout its history, Connecticut has depended on the energy and creativity of its many small companies to create products and jobs. Now, more than ever, our state needs and welcomes the efforts of entrepreneurs to help us compete in the nation and the world. I will continue my efforts to create an environment in Connecticut that is hospitable to business.

I am very pleased to acknowledge the important contribution of Community Accounting Aid And Services, Inc. and the Connecticut Small Business Development Center to Connecticut's small business community. In their fifteen year partnership of service, CAAS and CSBDC are proof positive of what can be accomplished when the private and public sectors work together for mutual benefit.

Lastly, I would like to acknowledge the contribution of the many CAAS volunteers. These dedicated CPAs have donated their financial and management skills and countless thousands of hours helping small companies to start-up or improve their business operations.

Sincerely,

Lowell P. Weicker, Jr.
Governor

FOREWORD

This book was written for people who are going into business for the first time, but many parts of it will be valuable information resources for experienced company owners. It is made available through Community Accounting Aid And Services, Inc. and the Connecticut Small Business Development Center. Every year, business counsellors from CAAS and CSBDC spend thousands of hours helping entrepreneurs through the challenges of starting their own companies. This has been one of their handbooks. Thousands of copies of earlier editions can be found in successful companies throughout the state.

We designed the content of this edition by asking two questions: *What topics do CAAS and CSBDC clients most often ask about?* and *What topics give small companies the most difficulty?* We then enlisted some of Connecticut's leading business advisors as authors. They drew on their extensive experience to put complex business concepts into practical, useful terms, and added many examples to illustrate their ideas.

Like many publications, this was the work of many people and was supported by many organizations. We gratefully acknowledge the contributions of the many sponsoring organizations, advisors, copyreaders, technical reviewers, administrators and others who made the book possible. The list, as complete as we could make it, appears below.

Connecticut Society of Certified Public Accountants
University of Connecticut
Zaiga L. Antonetti
Tricia M. Heldmann
John S. Purtill, III
Richard C. Rogers
Lorraine A. Martin, CPA
Sheila K. Garvy, CPA
Diana M. Saucier
Abigail L. Greco
Mark Zampino

TABLE OF CONTENTS

TABLE OF CONTENTS CONTINUED

Appendix

INTRODUCTION

At first glance, the Connecticut business climate seems to favor large companies. After all, many of the five hundred industrial giants on Fortune Magazine's annual company list have their headquarters in Connecticut. But, Connecticut's history of innovation also makes it a breeding ground for small businesses, even during tough economic times. The state boasts thousands of small businesses and thousands of new ones start up every year. Not all of those new businesses are successful. In fact, 75% of all businesses fail in their first year of operation.

Starting a successful business means more than having a good idea for a product or service. The idea must be planned, financed and brought to market. Then, if you want your company to become successful, you must have an information system that allows you to make good business decisions. And, you must comply with many tax and record-keeping rules. If you fail to do these things, you may make poor business decisions and you may have to pay extra taxes and penalties.

The purpose of this book is to help you to go from a good idea to a good business. It draws on the expertise of some of Connecticut's leading experts in business planning, accounting and taxes. These authors have used their experience in helping small businesses to bring you useful, practical advice on how to start up and run your business.

The material in the book is arranged in the order in which you'll use it to start your business, starting with writing a business plan. It takes you through deciding on the type of business, setting up business records, paying payrolls and finally, paying income taxes.

ORGANIZATION OF CHAPTER

Starting up a business
Why do people start small businesses?
Are you ready to run a small business?
Getting free help from CAAS

STARTING UP A BUSINESS

Appendix A, at the back of your book, is a checklist that shows the process you'll need to follow in setting up your business, once you've decided on what the business will be. This general checklist leads into other checklists for each chapter. This checklist emphasizes the six important success factors for small businesses:

1. Develop a business plan to guide you.

2. Have enough money available to start your business and to carry you through the start-up phase.

3. Select the right form of business organization and get it formed correctly.

4. Keep good business records.

5. Handle your tax obligations without paying too much or too little tax.

6. Market your company effectively.

WHY DO PEOPLE START SMALL BUSINESSES?

Everyone has a reason. More than any other reason, people start small businesses because they want the autonomy that goes with it. A recent survey summarizes the reasons:

Financial reasons, including earning more income and building personal wealth.	24%
Non financial reasons, including being self employed, autonomy, challenge, pursue an idea, use skills, no better alternatives, meet personal expectations, build an organization, gain respect or recognition, contribute to society, live in an area of choice or other reasons.	76%
Total	<u>100%</u>

ARE YOU READY TO RUN A SMALL BUSINESS?

Should you start up a small business? Maybe not. Running a small business isn't for everyone. Successful small businesses demand much from their owners. Many businesses fail because their owners don't have the right personality traits for the small business environment. This is a list of some of the personality traits the Small Business Administration says are important for small business owners:

Experienced   Having a management or supervisory background in the type of business being started.

Farsighted   Able to set goals and plan ahead.

Leader   Able to direct the activities of others and accept responsibility for the results.

Organizer   Able to develop and establish routines and procedures for efficient execution of plans.

Decision maker   Able to make decisions quickly and act on them.

Disciplined   Able to get things done on time.

Hard working   Willing to work long hours.

Motivated   Able to be a self-starter, without someone else to initiate actions.

Healthy   Having the stamina and energy to do everything that is required in the business.

Personable   Able to work with customers, employees and suppliers.

Adaptable   Willing to learn new techniques and procedures.

GETTING FREE HELP FROM CAAS

Community Accounting Aid and Services, Inc. (CAAS), is a not-for-profit organization supported by the accounting profession, the Connecticut Small Business Development Center (CSBDC) and by several Connecticut companies. CAAS consists of a full-time executive director and a network of CPAs and accountants who offer education services to all businesses and free professional services to *disadvantaged* businesses.

There are three ways to take advantage of CAAS services:

Education services
CAAS professionals conduct seminars throughout the state, in conjunction with the Connecticut Small Business Development Center and in adult education programs. Contact the CSBDC office for a schedule. There is usually a small charge for the seminars.

Accounting assistance
CAAS professionals provide a full range of accounting assistance, except for audits, to eligible disadvantaged businesses. To be eligible for this free service, a CAAS client must have less than $25,000 in net income or be a not-for-profit organization with an annual budget less than $100,000.

Workshops
CAAS professionals conduct free tax workshops and clinics. To find out about them, contact the CAAS office.

This book is one of CAAS' services to small business, too. Study it carefully and use it for reference. It was written by CPAs, lawyers and other business people who run successful companies and who help others to do so. It explains the many steps you must take to get started in business and to run your business. You must be prepared to take these steps if you want to be successful.

INTRODUCTION

This chapter discusses the process of business planning and shows a practical approach to business planning for small companies. The chapter is an adaptation for small companies of techniques that are effective in large companies.

Large companies devote considerable time to formal business planning. Their managers know they will not succeed unless they make ambitious plans and carry them out. Small companies owners should do formal business planning, too, if they want their companies to survive and prosper.

The most important time for business planning is before starting up. This planning allows the owners to make many crucial business decisions, including the decision of whether or not to go into business. A written business plan is essential when the owner must get financing to start in business because banks and investors will not advance money to a company without first studying its business plan. The plan is equally important for company owners that *do not* need financing, because it helps them decide if their money will be well spent and if they will have enough money to start up.

The techniques discussed in this chapter have been used by all types of companies for many years. They are used by CPA firms, the Small Business Administration (SBA), the Connecticut Small Business Development Center (CSBDC) and other consultants that advise small companies. This chapter contains an example of a business plan. This plan is only an illustration. Very likely, some lenders and investors will ask for more information than this one contains, because most of them have their own requirements for business plans. So, it is a good idea, before starting to work on a business plan, to discuss the contents with potential lenders and investors.

ORGANIZATION OF CHAPTER

Background of business planning
Time frames for business plans
Narrative part
Financial part

BACKGROUND OF BUSINESS PLANNING

Recent decades of business turbulence have proved the value of business planning. Before that, the owners of small companies relied on their instincts when making business decisions. They did not stray far from their basic lines of business, and the business climate was stable, so instinct worked well. However, modern managers have found they have to use business planning techniques to manage through the dramatic shifts and rapid changes that have occurred lately.

Some business owners can still rely on their instincts, if their companies are very well established and very stable. The rest of us have to devote more time to planning in order to keep pace with change.

The business plan, with its focus on strategy, has grown to be accepted and demanded by private investors, banks, governmental agencies, venture capitalists and others. They use it to measure the viability of existing or new ventures. But, the common perception that the prime purpose of a business plan is to get loans and investments is false. The real purpose is to help in making strategic business decisions.

Goals of Business Planning

Good business planning is an essential tool for success. Experience shows a strong connection between business planning and success. Good business planning allows management to:

■   Figure the amount of money needed to start up and continue in operation.

■   Estimate the company's future profits.

■   Decide on marketing strategies.

■   Identify opportunities to improve the business.

Unfortunately, many small business operators don't get around to developing business plans unless they are pushed to do so by their bankers or by prospective investors. For these operators, there is one additional goal: persuade investors or bankers to advance money to the company. Without this persuasion, they will not advance money.

Business Plan Contents

Most business plans have three parts:

Narrative	This part covers the company's purpose and descriptions of the various operating functions, (marketing, sales, organization & management, competition), followed by a summary.
Financial	This part presents balance sheets, operating and cash flow projections for at least one, but normally three to five years.
Appendix	This part contains statistical and reference material to support the first two parts. It also includes the resumes of the owners and top managers.

These three parts are the minimum content for a business plan. When it is used to support a financing request, the business plan is a sales tool. It also might include photographs, charts, graphs, product samples and other items to make the reader comfortable with the company and its plan.

TIME FRAMES FOR BUSINESS PLANS

A business plan should carry the reader about three years into the future. A typical plan might cover three different periods:

First Year	A one year outlook showing monthly financial detail for the first year of operation. Includes start-up costs and actions to achieve goals in the following years.
Next Two	A two or three year picture showing the effect of plans to achieve success as the company matures.
Later	A broad overview, in discussion form of general plans for the future. Includes dealing with the changing economy, introduction of new products and services, etc.

The first three years are the *make-or-break* years. If a company gets past them, its prospects are very good. The next three to five years determine whether a company has true staying power. If so, it can weather recessions, management changes, market changes and other adversity.

NARRATIVE PART

The narrative part is a brief description of the overall plan. It is important to strike a balance between too much and too little detail. If there is too much detail, nobody will read it. If the business plan is only an outline, a reader will think the owners haven't done enough planning. The language should be precise and the writing should flow easily from section to section.

A suggested structure for the narrative part is shown in the table below. A discussion of the subsections follows the table.

Section	Description	Pages
Introduction	Background of company, owners, products, industry.	1 to 1½
Business Purpose	Description of company's product or service.	¾ to 1
Marketing	Demographics of customers; approaches to selling; location of business; analysis of competition.	4 to 5
Organization	Company structure; assigned responsibilities; personnel needs.	1 to 2
Summary	Overview showing company's long term viability.	¾ to 1½

It's also a good idea to include a table of contents. An example appears on the facing page.

Hill Valley Amoco, Inc. Business Plan Example **Page 1**

Hill Valley Amoco, Inc.
Business Plan
Table of Contents

    *   Not included in this example due to space limitations.

Introduction Section

Entrepreneurs must recognize that many companies fail because the owners lack the experience and planning to implement their visions. Owners must be comfortable with their experience in the chosen business. This experience can come from various sources in several forms: the proposed line of business; related business fields; handling people (customers and employees); financial skills.

Most lenders and investors receive many business plans to read, and don't have time to study each one closely. In some business plans, these decision-makers never get past the introduction. If the purpose of the business plan is to raise money, the introduction must convince the reader that the plan is worth reading in full.

For new businesses, the introduction should tell why the owner decided to start the company. For mature companies, the introduction should tell a brief history. For all companies, the introduction should influence the reader to read the rest of the plan.

Hill Valley Amoco, Inc. Business Plan Example   Page 2

Introduction

Hill Valley Amoco is a complete travel services center proposed for the intersection of I-41 and I-42 in Hill Valley, Connecticut. The owner is an experienced service station manager who has worked in similar businesses for eight years and managed one for six years. He managed the North Avenue EXXON Service Center from construction to start-up and for two years after that. This highly successful business won the EXXON regional award for highest sales for both of those years. He has many skills for this business, including:

■   Product knowledge.
■   Management experience.
■   Business reputation.
■   Marketing knowledge.

The location for this business is ideal. It has a high traffic volume and easy highway access. The state only recently made the land available and the town does not allow travel services in this area, so there is very little competition. Initially, we plan to offer self service gasoline, car wash and a convenience store. Later, we plan to add light repairs and towing services.

The total funds needed for this business will be $800,000, including land and start-up cost. It will be provided as follows:

Owner's investment	100,000
Amoco expansion loan	150,000
SBA/Bank financing	550,000
Total cost	800,000

In developing this plan, the owner has consulted with a CPA, attorney, the Amoco marketing representative and the Hill Valley town planner. These consultations took place over the past two months and were finished in January, 1993. The following is an approximate timetable of events leading up to starting operations:

Complete business plan	January 31, 1993
Financing in place	May 1, 1993
Closing on land	May 15, 1993
Start construction	June 15, 1993
Complete construction	October 30, 1993
Initial opening	November 15, 1993
Grand opening	December 1, 1993

Business Purpose Section

For new companies, this section should broadly describe the company's products or services and market to which they will be offered.

Sometimes, it's helpful to describe the business using the Federal government's Standard Industrial Classification (SIC) code number. That's because many bank loan officers use published SIC data to validate information presented in a company's business plan. All companies fall into a SIC classification. For example, the SIC group for *Gasoline Service Stations* is *5541*. The SIC code number is used to classify statistical data on companies, including sales volume, numbers of companies and financial performance ratios.

The competitive market should be considered and identified. In every market, there are markets that are defined by a *quality-price-service* relationship. For example, the clothing industry has at least three competitive segments: high, medium and low. Some retailers occupy the high quality, high price and excellent personal service segment. Others compete at the intermediate level. Still others sell lower quality, lower price goods. The positioning within these markets is constantly being refined as competitors fight for customers and profits. *It is possible for a well-managed company to be successful in any one of the markets it chooses to occupy.*

For mature companies, the business purpose section of the narrative should discuss the company's history, considering changes in the economic environment, shifts in population, shifts in the customer base, shifts in the "quality-price-service" market and organizational problems.

Hill Valley Amoco, Inc. Business Plan Example **Page 3**

Background

This business is really three businesses in one: a gasoline station, a convenience store and a car wash. It offers expansion opportunities, too.

The gas station is a self-service facility offering three gasoline grades and diesel fuel. The convenience store is a 2,000 square foot store offering dairy products, small sizes of grocery products, quick meals and a large assortment of snack foods. The car wash is a cloth "tunnel" with wash, wax, underwash and vacuum, without a self-serve bay. The gas station and convenience store will operate 24 hours. The car wash will operate 10 hours.

This combination of businesses at one location should appeal to two types of customer: motorists traveling on I-41/I-42 and local residents. Motorists are attracted to a "one stop" business like this because they can save time while traveling. Local residents like it because they can purchase gas on the way to work and pick up milk and other small groceries or wash their cars on the way home.

When I-42 was designed, the State Highway Department planners decided not to include travel services, because the State had experienced difficulties with them in the past, and because the budget did not allow for the additional cost of exit and entrance ramps and buildings. This created a need for travel services in the I-41/I-42 interchange zone. However, the Hill Valley Town Council did not include travel services in the zoning plan for the interchange. As a result of consumer complaints in the past two years, the zoning plan will be amended to allow travel services starting April 1, 1993.

On learning about this change, the owner purchased an option to purchase the best piece of land in the area. This purchase locks out other possible competitors, because they may not get zoning approval, and they can't get the same oil company financing.

Marketing Section

Realistically speaking, small businesses rarely create new wants or needs. They normally fill existing wants and needs. Therefore, the first step in market planning is to define those in need of the product or service. This section of the plan is data-oriented, and owners should plan to get a solid command of the market numbers. These include:

■ Demographics of market, including size, description, location, growth rates, affluence, trends, etc.

■ Competition, including names, sizes, location, products, strategies, strengths, weaknesses, trends, etc.

The marketing section of the plan should be very specific about this market data. Being specific helps the owner to make better, more informed decisions. It also shows lenders and investors that the company is not relying on hunches, intuition, dreams or limited observations but rather depending on confirmed facts. There are two main types of market data:

Retail   The demographics for local areas or regions are available at chambers of commerce, the Connecticut Development Authority, CSBDC and other state departments. These demographic reports give a detailed composition of the population across several categories, such as education, sex, age, and income.

Wholesale   The demographic data for companies is arranged by Standard Industrial Classification numbers and can be secured from local, state, and national trade associations, regional and local chambers, state economic development offices and the federal department of commerce.

Marketing

In planning this enterprise, we have studied three factors:

- The local market.

- Marketing plans.

- Competition.

Local Market

The total traffic volume through the area has been estimated by town planners at 75,000 vehicles per day. In addition, there are approximately 15,000 people living within 5 miles of the proposed location. The local residents commute elsewhere to work and shop, because there are few local employers or retail stores. Therefore, we believe these residents are potential customers.

Oil company marketing representatives estimate this facility can support monthly self-service gasoline sales volume of 150,000 gallons. They also estimate monthly retail convenience store sales of $40,000. We have reduced these estimates to recognize that these sales might not materialize in the first three years, and that there may be competitive factors that reduce the sales.

An estimate of the sales and profit factors for the first year of business appears in the table in the financial section of the plan. The estimates assume the sales will grow from a modest level to maturity over about 2 years. This expectation has been verified with oil company representatives, who find the same pattern in similar start-ups.

Armed with the definition of the target market, management must develop plans to capture market attention. Generally, these plans include three items:

■   Type of sales organization (employees or agents).

■   Advertising plans, including company awareness and product advertising.

■   Promotion plans, including use of media for sales and promotional events.

The company's location is a key element of the market plan. The business plan should list the reason the company's location was chosen. Location should depend on the demographics of the target market and the nature of the product or service. Different factors are important for different types of companies. For a retail business, customer travel convenience and parking are key factors. For manufacturing companies, raw material supply, transportation, labor supply and customer locations are the major factors to be considered in site selection.

The final aspect of the market summary is the competitive analysis. All companies operate in a competitive marketplace. Competitive planning requires research on, and personal observation of, current and potential competitors. The competitive analysis should clearly define:

■   Total market potential for products or services.

■   Segment of market in which the company will operate.

■   Strategy to be used to penetrate the market.

■   Competitors.

■   Extent of market penetration projected for each year in the business plan, either in units or sales dollars.

New companies must consider all of these factors in developing their marketing program. However, existing companies need to be cautioned that past practices need to be reviewed in light of today's, not yesterday's, environment. Failure to make such a review leads to the ultimate failure of the planning process.

Hill Valley Amoco, Inc. Business Plan Example   **Page 5**

As the sales plan shows, there are seasonal patterns in sales. In winter months, people purchase less gasoline because they travel less. However, their cars get dirty from the dirt and salt from snow control operations and they use the car wash more. The convenience store sales show no seasonal pattern.

The profit margins were suggested by Amoco personnel. The actual retail gasoline price margin in this area varies from 9¢ to 15¢ per gallon. We have used 9¢ to recognize that we must keep prices low to attract new customers and to keep them until they have become loyal. We expect to raise the car wash prices an average of 10% in October before the next peak season. This would make the average sale $9.35. This increase may make customers reduce their consumption, so we reduced the average sale to $9.00.

Marketing Plans

These were suggested by our supplier. The supplier publishes a complete marketing manual, which contains advertising copy and marketing aids for typical dealers. We have followed the suggestions for a dealership of our size. After an initial rollout, which is included in the estimate of start-up costs, we will place regular advertisements in the *Shoppers World* and *Hill Valley Chronicle*. We also plan to distribute flyers on cars in parking lots and at public places. These flyers will carry discounts of up to 15% off regular retail prices.

The table below shows planned advertising costs. Like sales, these have a seasonal pattern.

Competition

We are in a competitive market, with eight self-service gas stations within five miles. However, only one has all three features on one site: gas, retail and car wash. Therefore, we expect to hold a reasonable market share.

The proposed location has superior visibility from one Interstate highway, because it sits at the top of an overpass. A normal sign can be seen from well before each exit ramp. No other station has that visibility. From the other Interstate highway, we must use billboard advertising to capture customers. We do not plan to use billboards until the third year.

Organization Section

This section discusses the company's legal structure, management assignments and similar issues.

The legal structure depends on tax, ownership and legal protection questions. The business plan should explain what structure was chosen and why. There are five ownership forms, which are discussed in Chapter 5:

- Sole Proprietorship.

- Partnership.

- Limited Liability Company.

- "S" Corporation.

- "C" Corporation.

The right choice of business organization depends on many factors, including the type of business, owners' financial situation, legal liability and plans for the future. The selection of a form of ownership should not be made casually. This important decision should be made only after consulting with both a CPA and an attorney.

The other organization issue is organizing the people. In small, owner-dominated companies, there is little doubt who is in charge. As the company grows, and needs more money, lenders and investors need to see that it has depth in personnel, and that the company could survive if the founder were not around. Thus, business plans for some companies should clearly define the top leadership positions and the responsibilities for each position.

To show the people organization, the business plan might also include a simple organization chart and brief descriptions of peoples' jobs. The job descriptions are especially helpful if the jobs are unusual. They also can be helpful in managing the business, and dealing with employees who need a lot of structure in their jobs. Conversely, they can be a handicap to an owner who wants an open, informal business atmosphere.

Hill Valley Amoco, Inc. Business Plan Example **Page 6**

Business Organization

Because of the tax advantages during start-up the company will be an "S" corporation. Initially, the owner will own all the shares. However, as the company grows and prospers, shares will be transferred to the owner's spouse and children. Practically all similar companies are organized as "S" corporations, because of the need for legal and environmental protection.

Personnel

The owner's resume is enclosed. His experience is extensive, and includes:

- Total experience of 8 years.
- Management experience of 6 years.
- Won EXXON regional award for highest sales for 2 years.
- Product knowledge.
- Management experience.
- Business reputation.
- Marketing knowledge.
- EXXON marketing training school.
- EXXON store management seminar.
- Graduate of Connecticut Technical School - mechanics.

The major organizational factor is the availability of workers for the business. As the chart below shows, we need over thirty workers to be able to provide 24 hour service. This includes shift leaders. We expect to recruit them in the local area, and believe the combination of high local unemployment and many young people will give us a reliable work force. The fact we can offer advancement into supervisory positions is an added incentive.

There are two aspects of organization that owners of start-up companies neglect: training and expansion. If new employees have to be trained, the business plan should say so and the company budget should include money for the training. Even on-the-job training costs money, because the people are getting paid when they aren't fully productive. If the business plan calls for growth, it should also plan for more people to handle the growth. The plan should identify the points at which new employees have to be added to handle the anticipated business.

The owner of a small company should consider the benefits of an advisory board. This is a panel of outside experts who serve as mentors, analysts, aides and sounding-boards. They advise on strategy and problem-solving. The advisors should be people whom the owner respects and can rely on to be open and candid, not "yes" people. Company owners should check with their trade associations for support, too. Many of them run support groups that meet regularly for discussion.

A final aspect of the company's organization is the source of its professional services. It is common for owners to rely on outside experts to guide them through regulatory and financial complexities. These would include lawyers, CPAs, environmental specialists and others. They should be named in the business plan. They should also be given copies of the complete plan for future reference.

Summary Section

The summary statement bridges the narrative and financial parts of a business plan when it is being submitted with a financing request. Typical themes for the summary include the following:

Market	Size of the total market, size of the company's target segment and projected growth. Information about basis for the projections.
Financial	Income, cash flow and balance sheet projections condensed and combined into a summary table. A possible format for the income summary is shown on the facing page.

Hill Valley Amoco, Inc. Business Plan Example   **Page 7**

Summary

Hill Valley Amoco, Inc. presents an excellent opportunity to provide travel services to an area that has none. The combination of an experienced owner/manager, outstanding location and superior marketing support from the supplier combine to give excellent chances of success.

Overview Of Financial Projections

	1994	1995	1996
Sales	968,773	1,065,650	1,172,215
Direct Costs	225,143	233,675	257,043
Gross Profit	743,630	831,975	915,172
Operating Expenses	706,043	739,915	776,110
Income from Operations	37,587	92,060	139,062
State Income Taxes	4,322	10,587	15,992
Net Income After Taxes	33,265	81,473	123,070

FINANCIAL PART

Bankers, investors and business owners use financial statements and accounting records to present information on operating results and as the basis for their business decisions. This chapter discusses them from a business planning point of view. A more detailed discussion appears in Chapter 7.

Financial statements are the tools used by the financial community to measure a company's financial health and viability. They are a major part of every business plan. Business owners need to understand them in order to communicate with bankers and investors and to chart the company's future.

The source records are not a formal part of the business plan. But, because they are the source of data for the statements, they have to be accurate. The quality of source records is a strong indicator of how well a business is run. Poor records usually mean poor management. Experienced investors know enough to look at a company's source records in order to form an opinion of how well it is being run.

The business plan should contain balance sheets, operating and cash flow statements. For a start-up company, they should show at least three future years. For a mature company, they should show two to three past years and five future years. For all companies, the first of the three years should be broken down into monthly periods. That is because the first year of a business plan has many fluctuations that do not show up in an annual statement. For illustration purposes, the examples in the next few sections present three year projections, without the monthly detail for the first year.

Proposed Funding

A good starting point for making a lender or investor understand a business venture is to express the amount of funds needed and to explain how they will be used. The table on the facing page is an example of how this is done.

Hill Valley Amoco, Inc. Business Plan Example | Page 8

Hill Valley Amoco, Inc.
Proposed sources and uses of funds

Sources:
  Owner's investment   100,000
  Amoco expansion advance   150,000
  SBA loan   550,000

Total   800,000

Uses:
  Purchase land   100,000
  Construction   400,000
  Inventory   80,000
  Furnishings   70,000
  Start-up costs   100,000
  Reserve for emergencies   50,000

Total   800,000

Projected Balance Sheets

The balance sheet reflects a company's financial condition at a specific moment in time by reporting what it owns, or assets, and what it owes, or liabilities. The term *balance sheet* refers to the fact that its two main components *balance*. The company's total assets equal the sum of its liabilities and its net worth. The table below defines the components.

Assets	Assets are the company's property, such as cash, inventory, furniture, motor vehicles, machines, computers and amounts receivable from customers. An asset is classified as *current* or *noncurrent* depending on whether it is converted into cash during the company's normal business operations cycle (usually one year). The company's inventories are current assets because they are sold to customers who pay for them in cash. Its furniture is a noncurrent asset, because it is normally not sold.
Liabilities	Liabilities are what the company owes to others, such as its unpaid bills, installment notes, unpaid payroll taxes and temporary advances from the owners. Like assets, liabilities are classified into current and noncurrent categories. But, for liabilities, a strict time frame is used. Current liabilities are those payable in less than one year from the date of the balance sheet. Noncurrent, or long term liabilities, are those payable after one year.
Net Worth	The company's net worth, or *equity,* is the balance left over after the liabilities are subtracted from the assets. This is the amount of the owners' investment in the company.

The format for the projected balance sheet in a business plan is similar to that of the usual balance sheet described in Chapter 7. The main differences are the number of time periods and the amount of detail presented in the business plan. The business plan statement presents three to five future years but in less detail than the normal company balance sheet.

The example on the facing page shows a projected balance sheet for our example, Hill Valley Amoco. This example shows the beginning position plus three yearly columns after that, but the owners could present any number of periods they choose.

Hill Valley Amoco, Inc. Business Plan Example | **Page 9**

Hill Valley Amoco
Projected Balance Sheet
December 31, 1994, 1995 and 1996

ASSETS

Assets:	1993	1994	1995	1996
Cash	100,000	40,399	32,431	41,176
Accounts receivable		50,000	50,000	50,000
Inventories	80,000	80,000	80,000	80,000
Prepaid items	20,000	20,000	20,000	20,000
Land	100,000	100,000	100,000	100,000
Building	400,000	400,000	400,000	400,000
Less accumulated depreciation	0	(20,000)	(40,000)	(60,000)
Equipment and improvements	70,000	70,000	70,000	70,000
Less accumulated depreciation	0	(8,750)	(17,500)	(26,250)
Organization costs	30,000	30,000	30,000	30,000
Less accumulated amortization	0	(6,000)	(12,000)	(18,000)
Total assets	800,000	755,649	712,931	686,926

LIABILITIES AND NET WORTH

Liabilities:	1993	1994	1995	1996
Accounts payable	0	22,385	23,194	24,119
SBA loan	550,000	500,000	425,000	325,000
Amoco expansion loan	150,000	100,000	50,000	0
Owner's loan	90,000	90,000	90,000	90,000
Total liabilities	790,000	712,385	588,194	439,119
Net worth:				
Capital stock	10,000	10,000	10,000	10,000
Retained earnings	0	33,264	114,737	237,807
Total net worth	10,000	43,264	124,737	247,807
Total liabilities and net worth	800,000	755,649	712,931	686,926

Note: This statement is included to illustrate the general principles of a balance sheet. A professionally-prepared statement is likely to contain more detail, more classification of amounts and extensive supplementary detail.

Projected Income Statements

Income statements report the company's revenue and expenses. The amount left over after expenses and income taxes is the company's *net income*. It isn't unusual for a company to lose money in the first year of start-up. This is because of start-up expenses and the fact that a newly-organized company is less efficient than a mature one.

The income statement projection in the example on the facing page shows a one part presentation where all income and expenses are combined on a single page. The income statement can also be presented in two parts: a summarized basic statement and a supporting schedule. The supporting schedule would present the details of operating and administrative expenses.

The projected income statement should be kept simple and clean. Investors and lenders need to be able to refer quickly to the basic financial information. This means moving the detail out of the main statement and into supporting schedules. An example of supporting schedules is shown on the pages that follow the income statement. They are the sales plan, marketing plan, and the employment plan. These plans cover the major elements of the income statement and show that the owner has done the necessary homework.

The projected statement of income, as well as other financial projections, is an excellent computer application. The planner who has access to a personal computer and simple software can try out different combinations to arrive at the best combinations. Available software includes commercial spreadsheet software such as Excel or Lotus 1-2-3. Software products designed specifically for business planning include Strategy Planner, Venture, Up Your Cash Flow and many others. The statement on the next page is an example of a projected income statement for a business plan that was prepared using a computer and spreadsheet.

The example presents gasoline profit as a single line, instead of two lines (revenues and costs). This is the preferred presentation for the retail gasoline industry.

Hill Valley Amoco, Inc.
Projected Income Statement
Years ended December 31, 1994, 1995, and 1996

	1994	1995	1996
Revenues:			
Gasoline profit	119,960	131,956	145,152
Convenience store	317,063	348,769	383,646
Car wash	531,750	584,925	643,418
Total revenues	968,773	1,065,650	1,172,215
Direct costs:			
Convenience store	212,432	233,675	257,043
Coupons redeemed	9,525		
Credit card discount	3,186		
Total direct costs	225,143	233,675	257,043
Gross profit	743,629	831,975	915,172
Expenses:			
Advertising	14,500	15,950	17,545
Depreciation	34,750	34,750	34,750
Insurance	10,250	10,250	10,250
Interest	56,000	53,200	50,540
Medical insurance	24,625	24,625	24,625
Owner's payroll taxes	9,000	9,750	10,500
Owner's salary	60,000	65,000	70,000
Payroll	320,363	336,382	353,201
Payroll service	2,500	2,500	2,500
Payroll taxes	48,055	50,458	52,982
Professional fees	5,000	5,250	5,513
Property taxes	20,000	21,000	22,050
Repairs	10,000	11,500	13,225
Supplies	6,000	6,000	6,000
Uniforms	2,000	2,000	2,000
Utilities, electric	50,000	55,000	60,500
Utilities, gas	10,000	11,000	12,100
Utilities, telephone	3,000	3,300	3,630
Utilities, water	20,000	22,000	24,200
Total expenses	706,043	739,915	776,110
Profit before income taxes	37,586	92,060	139,062
State income tax	4,322	10,587	15,992
Federal income tax	n/a	n/a	n/a
Net income after taxes	33,264	81,473	123,070

Note: This simplified income statement has been included to illustrate the general principles of an income statement. A professionally-prepared income statement is likely to have different categorizations and details.

Hill Valley Amoco, Inc. Business Plan Example — Page 11

Hill Valley Amoco, Inc.
Sales Plan

	Gasoline			Retail			Car Wash		
	Sales	Margin	Profit	Sales	Margin	Profit	Number	Price	Amount
Jan-94	100,000	0.09	9,000	25,000	0.33	8,250	6,000	8.00	48,000
Feb-94	100,000	0.09	9,000	25,250	0.33	8,333	6,000	8.00	48,000
Mar-94	105,000	0.09	9,450	25,503	0.33	8,416	5,500	8.00	44,000
Apr-94	105,000	0.09	9,450	25,758	0.33	8,500	5,000	8.00	40,000
May-94	115,500	0.09	10,395	26,015	0.33	8,585	5,000	8.00	40,000
Jun-94	121,275	0.09	10,915	26,275	0.33	8,671	5,000	8.00	40,000
Jul-94	121,275	0.09	10,915	26,538	0.33	8,758	5,000	8.50	42,500
Aug-94	121,275	0.09	10,915	26,803	0.33	8,845	4,500	8.50	38,250
Sep-94	115,211	0.09	10,369	27,071	0.33	8,934	5,000	8.50	42,500
Oct-94	109,451	0.09	9,851	27,342	0.33	9,023	5,000	9.00	45,000
Nov-94	109,451	0.09	9,851	27,616	0.33	9,113	5,500	9.00	49,500
Dec-94	109,451	0.09	9,851	27,892	0.33	9,204	6,000	9.00	54,000
Total	1,332,888		119,960	317,063		104,631	63,500		531,750

Hill Valley Amoco, Inc.
Marketing Plan

	Newspaper	Flyers	Discounts	Total
Jan-94	1,000	500	900	2,400
Feb-94	1,000	500	900	2,400
Mar-94	500	500	825	1,825
Apr-94	500	500	750	1,750
May-94	500	500	750	1,750
Jun-94	500	500	750	1,750
Jul-94	500	500	750	1,750
Aug-94	500	500	675	1,675
Sep-94	500	500	750	1,750
Oct-94	1,000	500	750	2,250
Nov-94	1,000	500	825	2,325
Dec-94	1,000	500	900	2,400
Total	8,500	6,000	9,525	24,025

Hill Valley Amoco, Inc. Business Plan Example　　　　**Page 12**

Hill Valley Amoco, Inc. Employment Plan			
	Full-time	Part-time	Total
Jan-94	15	11	26
Feb-94	15	12	27
Mar-94	15	12	27
Apr-94	15	11	26
May-94	15	10	25
Jun-94	15	10	25
Jul-94	15	10	25
Aug-94	15	11	26
Sep-94	16	11	27
Oct-94	16	11	27
Nov-94	16	13	29
Dec-94	17	14	31
Average	15.4	11.3	26.7
Average hours per week	40	10	
Average wage	8.75	6.75	
Total	280,583	39,780	320,363

Projected Cash Flow Statements

Balance sheets and income statements show only two parts of the company's financial picture. Their limitation is that they don't present a complete cash picture. They do not provide information concerning the varying cash needs of the company. Cash flow statements were designed to fill that void.

The cash flow statement presents the flow of funds needed to support the business. It projects the receipts and payments, adds them to the opening cash balance and projects the closing cash balance. This statement tells the owners whether they need to borrow or invest more money to stay in business.

If the cash flow projection shows a shortage, the business plan must show how the shortage will be covered. If there is surplus cash, the plan should show it being invested in the business or paid back to lenders and investors.

The example on the opposite page shows an example of a three year cash flow projection.

Assumptions

In order to prepare financial projections, we have to make assumptions about inflation, tax rates, population and many other items. The business plan should present these assumptions in a summarized form to help the reader understand the plan better, and believe it. The table in the facing page shows the typical assumptions that would have to be made in order to prepare a business plan.

Hill Valley Amoco, Inc. Business Plan Example   **Page 13**

Hill Valley Amoco
Summary of Planning Assumptions
Years ended December 31, 1994, 1995 and 1996

	1994	1995	1996
Depreciation life (years) - Building	20	20	20
Depreciation life (years) - Equipment	8	8	8
Receivable turns per year (house accounts)	12.0	12.0	12.0
Inventory turns per year (convenience sales)	4.0	4.5	5.0
Payable Turns per year	12.0	12.0	12.0
Interest Rate % - SBA debt	9.00%	9.00%	9.00%
State Tax Rate %	11.50%	11.25%	11.00%

No federal income tax is included because the Corporation is an "S" corporation and pays only state income taxes.

No projection for inflation has been included in any of the numbers in this business plan.

Hill Valley Amoco
Cash Flow Projection
Years ended December 31, 1994, 1995 and 1996

	1994	1995	1996
Net income after tax	33,264	81,473	123,070
Add: Depreciation	34,750	34,750	34,750
	68,014	116,223	157,820
Less Increase in accounts receivable	(50,000)	0	0
Add Increase in accounts payable	22,385	808	925
Cash flow from operations	40,399	117,031	158,745
Less SBA loan payments	(50,000)	(75,000)	(100,000)
Less Amoco loan payments	(50,000)	(50,000)	(50,000)
Less owner loan payments	0	0	0
Net cash flow	(59,601)	(7,969)	8,745
Opening cash	100,000	40,399	32,431
Ending cash	40,399	32,431	41,176

Note: This simplified cash flow statement has been included to illustrate the general principles of a cash flow statement. A professionally-prepared statement is likely to contain considerably more detail.

Start-up Expenses

Before a company can even open its doors, it has to buy furniture and equipment, make security deposits and go through a period when there are expenses but no revenues. These costs have to be figured in the business plan, but many small business owners either forget them or underestimate them. One way to get a list of the equipment needs is to take a mental walk through the office, store or factory, listing everything in sight. Another is to consult with financial advisors and others who have started their own companies. A third way is to use a checklist like the one in Appendix K.

For more discussion of start-up costs, see Chapter 6 on raising capital.

Hill Valley Amoco, Inc. Business Plan Example	Page 14

Hill Valley Amoco, Inc.
Start-up Expenses

Advertising for grand opening	10,000
Training payroll during start-up	20,000
Discount program	10,000
Stationery and office supplies	4,000
Decorations	10,000
Professional fees	10,000
Bank loan closing fees	30,000
Miscellaneous	6,000
Total	100,000

CONCLUSION

Business planning is not just for big companies. A business plan, and the business planning process, are essential to *any* company's success. The process is detailed, but it pays off in better chances for success.

The business plan consists of a combination of written material and analytical data. A good business plan covers all aspects of running the business: product, service, customers, market, competition, type of business organization, personnel and financing. This broad coverage, and the discipline of preparing the plan stimulates the owner to decide on business strategies and to be realistic about financing needs and growth prospects.

Chapter 3
Effective Marketing

INTRODUCTION

This chapter discusses marketing topics from the perspective of small start-up companies. Like their counterparts in large companies, managers of small ones must use the two main tools of marketing: research and planning. However, they have the advantage of being closer to their customers, and they should exploit that advantage.

One goal of marketing for small businesses is to bring about objective decision-making in an area where the decision-making often is instinctive and short-sighted. The business owner's excitement and enthusiasm are positive forces when they can be combined with solid market research and logical planning. The marketing concepts in this chapter have been specially adapted to small businesses. They apply to the start-up phase or to the management of ongoing activities and expand on the brief reference to marketing in Chapter 2.

The techniques discussed in this chapter apply to both of the major marketing fields: *consumer marketing*, where the retail customer is the target and *business-to-business marketing*, where business customers are the target. Many of the marketing concepts and strategies used for each are similar, but the seller must use separate marketing programs for each customer group.

The chapter follows the development of effective marketing, starting with identifying the customer, to strategies to increase sales.

ORGANIZATION OF CHAPTER

Defining the customer
Getting information about the market
Estimating market size
Differentiating a company from competitors
Choosing a retail location
Setting selling prices
Advertising
Keeping customers satisfied
Increasing sales

DEFINING THE CUSTOMER

The purpose of marketing and the marketing plan is to understand the customer's needs and decide how best to attract and serve that customer. This starts with describing the customer. Many business people can't describe their best customers, so a business manager who can describe them has a definite edge. The customer definition process can take the form of questions, the more the better. The goal is to identify the target customer and learn what's important to that customer. Examples of questions are:

- What kinds of people do I want to sell to?

- What are their annual incomes?

- How far away from my store or business do they live?

- How old are they?

- What are their occupations?

- Are they married or single?

- Do they have children? How many?

- What are their shopping habits?

- What are their likes and dislikes?

- What do they read?

- What do they do for entertainment?

- How important is cost of service to them?

- How important is quality of service? Timeliness of service?

- Why would they use my product or service instead of a competitor's?

This type of questioning is introspective, and the answers are influenced by the manager's own attitudes. For example, a 30 year old manager may see all customers as 30 years old, when the best target customers might be 40 years old or 20 years old. So, for more objective customer definition, larger established companies use surveys and interviews to help them define the customer base more objectively.

GETTING INFORMATION ABOUT THE MARKET

Once the customer is defined, the next step is to get more information. For this objective, there is no substitute for market research. Research replaces hopes and opinions with facts. The research gathers information about three broad areas:

■ Market size, behavior, location and potential market share.

- Where are these customers found?

- How do they make their purchase decisions?

- What is the total market size for the products or services?

- How much market share is realistically attainable?

■ Competition.

- What competitors are trying to attract the same customers?

- What are the competitors' strategies in pricing, packaging, and location?

- What are the competitors' market shares and trends in the marketplace?

- What are the competitors' strengths and weaknesses?

■ Competitive positioning.

- What percentage of the market is available for capture?

- Is the business well-located?

- Is the product or service priced correctly?

- Does the packaging or method of delivery suit the customer's needs?

Fortunately, most of this market research can be done by the business owner without the help of paid professionals. While professional help is readily available, it is generally expensive. Many of the above questions can be answered by using common sense coupled with information that already exists.

Market size issues are discussed in more detail in the section entitled *Estimating Market Size*.

Formal Sources of Information

There are several sources of reliable, current market information. These include:

Trade associations — These organizations represent specific industries and are a good source of information and support. Most trade associations publish data on their industries and make that data available to members. The names of trade associations can be found in a library. Two publications include the *Encyclopedia of Trade Associations* and the *Connecticut State Register and Manual*. Both are updated annually.

Chambers of commerce and local economic development officers — Local chamber offices can provide local population information, zoning regulations, maps and lists of other local business. In addition, they can lead to other information resources.

U. S. Census Bureau and Connecticut's Department of Economic Development — Both agencies publish great quantities of economic data. Besides population data, the Census Bureau publishes specific trade and industry data. This information is available through local public libraries, through the Connecticut Small Business Development Center (CSBDC), or from the U. S. Department of Commerce, Bureau of the Census, Washington DC. 20230.

Public libraries — Many books, magazines, and government publications are available in the public library along with assistance in locating available resources.

Newspapers — Local and regional newspapers are an excellent source of information on local business news, town planning and zoning issues, local economic conditions and of course, a chance to study advertising placed by the competition.

Yellow Pages — This is a good source for competitive information, because most competitors are listed, and many take out display ads telling more about themselves.

Informal Sources of Information

One effective way to get good market information is to communicate directly with potential customers or with others who either know the market or represent the market. These sources can give invaluable insight into customer attitudes, market conditions and competition. And, they are inexpensive sources of market information. Some of these sources are:

Customers	This is where small business owners have an advantage over their large company counterparts. They are closer to customers and are better able to get market information from them. As the company grows, the best strategy for a small company manager is to remain close to the customers.
Suppliers	Suppliers communicate with many competitors and also with customers. They are an excellent source of information about business conditions, customers, market trends and competitors.
Competitors	Surprisingly, competitors are very willing to share information about market and product developments. This is especially true of companies that are close, but not direct, competitors.
Employees	Customers often say things to employees that they would not dare to say to company managers or owners. Employees should be encouraged to become friendly with customers and seek information about the company's performance and competitive actions.
Local business owners	These non-competing business operators are excellent sources of information about general business conditions. The chamber of commerce is the best place to meet them.
Counterparts in other markets	Suppliers and trade associations are quite willing to help business owners to network with their counterparts in other states. A successful counterpart is one of the best sources of ideas to improve business operations.

The drawback of all these sources is that they're not objective. All their information contains some degree of bias that has to be filtered out. Here are some examples of this bias:

■ Customers may complain about prices if they think their complaints can influence prices. But, price may not be a significant consideration in the customer's purchasing decision compared to others such as quality, delivery and other factors the customers take for granted.

■ Suppliers may add their own slant to market trend information. They may exaggerate estimates of demand in hopes of influencing a customer to increase purchases.

One way this information is gathered is by surveys. However, this is one area of research that shouldn't be a do-it-yourself project. It is best left to professionals who have been trained in the research techniques used in this highly specialized field. Questionnaire writing is much more complex than it looks. The way a question is worded, which questions are asked - and even which questions are not asked - can elicit worthless or misleading information that may lead to poor business decisions. Done properly, however, surveys can generate information needed for the business and can be the best source of information available.

Research isn't just for new businesses. It should be used periodically by established businesses as well. It can answer many questions when business is not going well, when a new competing product is introduced into the market, or when a new competitor comes into the market. It will keep existing businesses on target with their marketing plan and in tune with changing customer needs.

ESTIMATING MARKET SIZE

One of the biggest mistakes a business manager can make is to misjudge the size of a market. Estimate too high and there isn't enough sales volume to stay in business; estimate too low and customers are dissatisfied when they can't get service. To avoid these predicaments, all business managers must answer this critical question: "How many customers are out there who will want my product or service?" The answer to this question can come from careful research.

In judging markets, three concepts are important: potential market, served market and market share.

■   *Potential market* is the total number of customers who could possibly become customers for a product. This is an interesting but misleading piece of information. Many people who plan business operations rely too much on their estimates of the potential market. In their optimism, they think that every customer in a market is a real customer. But, it's not true. The fact is that many customers in a market just aren't going to buy from any source at any price.

■   *Served market* is the number of customers who are real buyers in a market or market segment. This is the most meaningful statistic for market planning, because it represents real customers.

■   *Market share* is the percentage of the customers in the served market who do business with a company or who can reasonably be expected to do business. This is a measure of the extent of competition, and the company's success in competing. Market share is never 100%, unless the company enjoys a monopoly.

    EXAMPLE

    To illustrate, assume you publish a newspaper in a town that has 20,000 families. Of them, 5,000 families don't subscribe to any newspaper, 5,000 subscribe to your newspaper, and only a very few subscribe to more than one newspaper. In this case, the *potential market* size is 20,000, the *served market* size is 15,000 (20,000 families minus the 5,000 who don't subscribe to any newspaper). You have a *market share* of 33⅓% (your 5,000 divided by the 15,000 served market).

In developing the business plan, served market and market share are critical success factors. In planning the entry into a market, the first step is to estimate the served market. The second is to figure how, and how soon, the company's market share can advance from zero to an acceptable level.

In business planning, market share is figured from the company's sales and the size of the served market. So, the first step is to figure the size of the served market. Rough estimates of the served market are adequate. So are estimates that are expressed as a high and low range.

There are three methods to estimate the size of a served market:

■ Guesses, hunches or personal experience.

■ Published information sources.

■ Customer surveys.

Guesses or hunches

This is the least scientific method to forecasting the size of a market, but it can be a reliable method if it's done by an expert. And every field has its experts. These are people who thoroughly understand the demographics of the market and have first-hand experience in the market. They can be hired from universities or companies in the industry, and there are many who operate as free-lance consultants. Most of them can be located through trade associations, trade conventions, and advertising or articles in trade magazines.

Besides market size information, an expert can provide this information:

■ Where to locate.

■ The geographic definition of the market.

■ The distance a customer will travel to make a purchase.

■ The distance the owner can travel to sell or service a product.

Once the served market is identified, the company is structured to fit into it and the development of the marketing strategy continues.

Published Information Sources

This involves using information that is available to the public. The benefit of these sources is that they are accurate and free. The main sources were listed in the table on Page 3-4. Most of this economic data covers total markets, so it has to be adjusted before it can be used as an estimate of the served market.

Surveys

For business-to-business marketing, published data isn't as pinpointed as survey data. Normally, the best approach is to ask customers about their buying habits and other information needed for market planning. Either telephone surveys or mail surveys are effective. The limitations of surveys for planning were discussed earlier. The data is likely to be unreliable unless the survey is done carefully.

When the market size data is assembled and evaluated it's time for a serious question: "Considering served market size and competitors, is it feasible to continue." The answer is "Yes" if the market is large enough, the competitive situation allows for another competitor and the product or service is needed. If the answer is "Yes," the next step is to determine how to compete in the market.

DIFFERENTIATING A COMPANY FROM COMPETITORS

Leading marketing authorities say one of the most effective competitive strategies is for a company to *differentiate* itself. This means finding things that make the company different from its competitors and to point out the differences to customers.

The goals of differentiation are to offer the customer a better value, and to help the customer make a more informed purchasing decision. Through differentiation, customers are attracted to a company's products or services, even if they're sold for a premium price. Through differentiation, a competitor gains market share and sells at a more profitable price. In many cases, the differences among competitors aren't real; in these cases differentiation becomes a matter of promotion.

There are four basic rules for differentiation:

- *The more similar a product is to that of a competitor, the more important differentiation becomes.* The goal is to turn a commodity into a unique product that is more desirable than those of competitors.

■ *If the company's goal is to get into a particular market, the product should be differentiated for that market.* This implies that no other product is suitable for the market.

■ *The first competitor that claims a feature gains an advantage.* If you claim your product has a special feature, a competitor would be making a mistake merely to claim the same feature. The competitor must now claim an additional feature to even the score. That may not be possible without revamping the product.

■ *Service providers, most of all, must differentiate themselves.* This is because a service is an intangible, which can't be seen, and it is difficult for customers to tell the difference from competitors' services.

These are a few of the many examples of differentiation:

■ A gasoline manufacturer claims its gas burns clean, even though it comes from the same refinery as other manufacturers' gas.

■ An apparel manufacturer advertises its products are made in the USA, even though many others are, too.

■ A floppy disk manufacturer claims its product is *for government or educational use only*, even though it's identical to those sold for other markets.

■ An insurance company claims you're in good hands, implying you're not in good hands with other insurance companies.

Differentiation strategies are limited only by the imagination. The process is to configure the product so that it's different (and therefore better) or find a way to claim that it is. The table below shows some ways this can be done. References to products also apply to services.

Quality	Offer highest quality
	Provide higher performance
Service	Offer fast service.
	Offer free delivery.

Custom offering	Vary the product to give customers a choice of colors, brands, styles, sizes.
	Offer customization of the product.
	Bundle another product with the basic product for the same price or 1¢ more.
	Include more product at the same price as the regular sized product.
	Use a different product package or display.
Location	Use different distribution channels to move the product to the market.
Price	Discounting, coupons, volume discounts
Advertising	Use advertising to point out product differences.
	Use different advertising media.

CHOOSING A RETAIL LOCATION

Marketing professionals say there is only one truly important factor for retail stores: location. The choices cover a broad range:

■ Central business district, or downtown area.

■ Mall.

■ Regional shopping center.

■ Small shopping strip.

■ Area heavily concentrated with a combination of shopping and commercial activity.

The major difference among these choices is the *traffic count*, or number of customers that travel through, and *type of traffic*, or the likelihood the travelers are customers.

Both are important factors in deciding on the location.

> *EXAMPLE*
>
> Large numbers of cars and pedestrians pass through downtown areas, but many of them are traveling to work or school and may not be prospective customers. But, of the many people who go to shopping malls, most are customers, because they have come to the mall to make purchases.

Deciding on the location is primarily a matter of trading off between several factors:

- *Traffic counts and rents.* As a rule, high traffic counts translate into high rents.

- *Competitors.* The issue isn't as easy to decide as it seems. Having a competitor close by can be an advantage or disadvantage. The nearby competitor will divert business, but it could mean a location is good for the type of business.

- *Complementary stores.* These are stores that draw traffic for each other. Today's customers want *one stop* shopping, where they can park and do all their shopping or errands in one location, without driving to another. Examples of complementary businesses are those on someone's Saturday errand list: dry cleaner, gas station, liquor mart, drug store, convenience store and supermarket.

Retailers can assess a particular store's effectiveness by looking at four indicators:

- Number of people passing by on an average day.

- Percentage who enter stores.

- Percentage who buy something.

■   Average amount spent per sale.

A store that is doing poorly might be in a poorly trafficked location, or not have enough drop-in traffic, or too many drop-ins who browse but do not buy, or do not buy very much. Each problem can be remedied. Traffic is remedied by a better location; drop-ins are increased by better window displays and sale announcements; the number buying and amount purchased depend on employee sales skills, merchandise quality and prices.

SETTING SELLING PRICES

Pricing a product or service is another crucial step for the business. Price too high and no one will buy. Price too low and there won't be enough profit to support the business in the long run. For large companies, product pricing is a major preoccupation. It should be for small companies, too. However, experience shows that small company managers don't take advantage of opportunities to improve pricing strategy and profits. Some of them are listed in the table below.

■   *Avoid relying too much on competitors to set selling prices.* Too often managers ask what prices their competitors are asking and set prices at the same - or lower - levels. This may not be the best strategy. For one thing, competitors may have different costs. For another, following the competition ignores the opportunity to practice differentiation. It may be a good idea to set prices higher than the competitors to differentiate from them.

■   *Don't confuse profit and markup percentages.* Markup and profit are one and the same: the amount added to cost to arrive at a selling price. However, as a percentage, markup is measured against cost while profit is measured against selling price.

EXAMPLE

A scarf costs $3.00 and sells for $5.00. Both the markup and the profit are $2.00. The markup percent is 66⅔% ($2.00 ÷ $3.00) and the profit percent is only 40% ($2.00 ÷ $5.00).

The confusing custom of using two different bases to figure the same profit can lead to bad decisions. If the goal were to earn a 40% profit, it wold be a mistake to add 40% on top of cost. That would give a profit of $1.20 (40% X $3.00), less than was needed.

The table below compares common markup and gross profit percentages:

Markup	Profit
200%	66⅔%
100%	50%
50%	33⅓%
25%	20%
11%	10%

■ *Avoid pricing strictly on cost.* Cost may not be the best basis for deciding on prices. One basis for pricing is demand. The higher the demand, the higher the price should be. Determine which products are selling and see if they are underpriced.

■ *Learn which products are price-sensitive.* Products that affect the customer's budget, like food, or are highly visible, like gasoline, are price sensitive. That is, customers will decide not to buy them if prices are raised even a small amount. A company that sells price-sensitive products has two options:

   ● Watch competitive prices carefully and avoid getting too far ahead of the market price.

   ● Differentiate the product, so the customer is able to recognize its value.

ADVERTISING

Advertising informs customers of the availability, desirability, and uses of a product. It also tries to convince customers that the company's products are superior to those of competitors. Every company must make three decisions about advertising:

■   How much money to spend.

■   Where to spend the money.

■   What to say in the advertisements.

This section covers the first two decisions. The last issue, about what to say in advertisements, is beyond the scope of this chapter, but was discussed in the earlier section on differentiation. An essential function of advertising is to reinforce the company's differentiation and features of products, then communicate to customers - repeatedly if possible.

Budgeting Advertising Dollars

Dollars are generally a scarce commodity in a new business, and budgeting them carefully helps ensure that advertising dollars are spent effectively. The idea of budgeting is to set aside a fixed annual sum for advertising and spread that amount - no more, no less - over the year. The budget helps remove some of the temptation to make impulse advertising purchases. A sure way to overspend on advertising is to leap at every chance to place an ad.

There are three ways advertising budgets are figured:

Percentage of sales	The company allocates a percentage of annual sales to advertising. As sales increase, the ad budget is also increased.
Unit of sales	The company sets aside a fixed sum for each unit of product or service sold.
Judgement	The owner decides how much to spend based on knowledge, experience or intuition.

One disadvantage of the first two methods is that advertising is cut when sales drop. But when sales levels fall advertising should probably be increased, not decreased, to get sales back on track. A cut in advertising may lead to further reductions in sales producing a downward trend for the company.

The percentage of sales method is the most popular for small companies. The percent can be set by trial-and-error or can be based on the amount spent by similar businesses. Industry statistics on advertising spending vary by the size of the business and can be found in trade magazines and independent data reports. One popular source is the Almanac of Business & Industry Ratios which publishes summary data by standard industrial classification (SIC code) to use for comparison. Below are a few examples of advertising expenditures, expressed as a percentage of sales, from the Almanac:

- General merchandise   2.6 - 3.4%

- Hardware & garden store   1.0%

- Apparel & accessory store   2.5 - 6.0%

- Contractors/developers   0.5%

- Restaurants   2.0 - 4.0%

- Personal service companies   2.0 - 5.0%

Deciding where to spend advertising money

There is a wide range of advertising mediums, and a wide range prices, too. Pick the wrong medium, and the advertising money is likely wasted. The challenge is to select the right medium for the company. Each medium has its advantages and disadvantages; some work well for one type of customer or product but not for others.

Some experimentation may be necessary to find the best advertising mix. The key to measuring the success is to track the results and spend advertising dollars on those programs that seem to work.

Sometimes not advertising at all is the right strategy. That's because the most effective medium for a small business is word-of-mouth advertising from satisfied customers. Many small companies choose not to advertise, or to do very little advertising, because they get enough benefit from word-of-mouth.

If advertising is necessary, choosing wisely is important. Although a small company could use the same advertising tools used by large companies, there are several that have proved to be the most effective:

- Radio and television.
- Newspapers.
- Direct mail and fliers.
- Yellow pages.
- Promotion.

Radio and television

These are best for selling consumer products, but not good for business-to-business selling.

Radio and television are the most successful media for selling to teenagers and young adults. The drawback of both is that the advertising message has a fleeting "shelf life." The message goes out and then it no longer exists. To be effective, the message has to be repeated until it sinks into the customer's memory. One strategy used by advertisers is called "pulsing." The ad is repeated for several days or weeks, then given a rest. After the rest, another pulse of ads is broadcast. This cycling continues as long as the advertiser chooses.

Television is associated with high cost advertising by large companies, and considered too expensive for many small firms to use. And that's true of major network stations. However, cable TV systems and low power TV stations, broadcasting only 15 to 25 miles, charge rates that are low enough for small companies.

Newspapers

Display ads in the local newspapers are generally effective for reaching retail customers in towns with total newspaper circulation of 50,000 or less. They tend not to be effective for business markets. A potential advertiser should talk with other small business advertisers about the effectiveness of display advertising and what days are most productive. For example, Wednesday and Sunday are the traditional days for food retailers to advertise in newspapers.

Newspaper shelf life is short, but it's longer than that of radio and TV. Local, weekly papers have the longest shelf life. Their market is also more geographically targeted, so they may represent a good newspaper value.

Direct mail and fliers

These are excellent for reaching business and retail customers, because they can be targeted. The cost per address of direct mail is higher than for radio, TV or newspapers because of the cost of postage and printing the promotion material. However, computer technology makes it possible to mail a message directly to a very narrow audience, making the expenditure more effective.

Yellow pages

Yellow page advertising is most effective for special products, services, and repair shops that potential customers will seek out. It is most effective for business selling. The shelf life of the yellow pages is the longest of all advertising methods - it lasts a full year. But, once in print, the message can't be changed.

Promotion

This includes specialty gifts imprinted with the company's name and telephone number and public relations advertising such as sports team sponsorship. Normally, these can't be the centerpiece of an advertising program, but can reinforce other advertising.

Using Advertising Agencies

Professional advertising firms are out of reach for most small companies because of high cost. However, many free-lance artists and writers are available to assist with advertising copy at prices that are much lower than those of professional advertising agencies. These people are found through the yellow pages, referrals from other small companies and from the local chamber of commerce.

Do-it-yourself advertising is popular with small companies. Only those owners who truly are creative should attempt it, however, because a poorly designed advertisement can create a poor image and do more harm than good for business.

For home-grown ad writers, there are three suggestions:

- Purchase a book (or books) on how to preparing advertising copy.

- Solicit objective criticism from a business counselor, trusted advisor or from customers.

- Measure the results from the home-grown ad. If it doesn't draw business quickly, don't take a chance. Cancel it and have one prepared by a professional.

KEEPING CUSTOMERS SATISFIED

Most owners want their companies and profits to grow. For this to happen, sales must increase. To many, this means they must get new customers while retaining their old customers. And, they feel they must then aggressively seek out new customers.

However, experience shows the opposite is true: ample growth can come just from the existing customer base. To successful companies, the best customer is a repeat customer. *They find that an overwhelming part of their growth is from existing customers and only a very small part is from new customers.*

So, the best growth strategy seems to be the one that concentrates on existing customers. This includes these actions:

- *Stress quality.* A strategy of quality improvement aims at increasing the functional performance of the product or service - its durability, reliability, speed, taste, etc. A small business owner can often overtake its competition by launching a new and improved product or service. The strategy is effective to the extent that the quality is improved and buyers accept the claim of improved quality.

■   *Emphasize service.* Many successful companies today have shifted their emphasis from sales to sales and service. Customer service has become an integral part of the sales package. The front line employees in these companies are trained to sell the product and also to service the customer. A happy customer is a repeat customer.

■   *Handle complaints properly.* The best advertising is word of mouth. Studies show that if a complaining customer is handled properly, the customer will go on to tell an average of five other customers about the positive experience. And a dissatisfied customer will tell up to fourteen potential customers about the unpleasant experience!

These actions can turn a dissatisfied customer into a cooperative one:

●   Let the customer fully air the complaint.

●   Don't interrupt or argue with the customer.

●   Ask how the problem can be resolved.

●   Take prompt action.

●   If possible, over-service the customer the next time around.

INCREASING SALES

The previous section discussed ways to grow by servicing existing customers. For many successful companies, that is the sole growth strategy. But what if that's not enough growth? That means getting many more new customers. And a somewhat different strategy.

First, remember that bigger doesn't always mean better, often it just means bigger. Before starting a strong burst of growth, ask if the growth is both justified and manageable. During the 1980s, many small service companies grew for the sake of growth. They suffered for the growth by having to shrink or go out of business in the 1990s.

Some good reasons to expand a small business include these:

■ Provide career opportunities for employees.

■ Improve customer service levels.

■ Retain customers who demand a broader range of products and services.

■ Improve personal income and net worth.

The expansion strategies for the 1990s are expected to be much different from those that worked during the 1980s. That's because the customer base has become more wary and more conservative. For the next decade, these strategies show the most promise:

■ *Specialize.* Experts predict that the business winners in the 1990s will be those that specialize. The business successes of tomorrow will be smaller companies that have highly skilled workers, who can always find ways to improve their product and production. They will service narrow market niches and produce quality products.

■ *Remain flexible.* The chief characteristic of a successful company will be (and always has been) flexibility. Market segmentation demands an agility to keep pace with the market niche. Smaller companies are proving that small size allows them to make changes quickly to respond. Competition will come from entrepreneurs that are niche marketers, seeing a product or service market that is not well served and going after it rapidly.

■ *Continue to think small.* Direct new product programs to small busines-ses. Don't launch a product or service by trying to sell big-name customers. Big companies take too long to make decisions, particularly about new or innovative products or services. Evidence shows that smaller companies make decisions more quickly, because they have fewer levels of management.

■ *Make everyone a sales person.* Start selling at the receptionist desk. Many low-level employees, such as the receptionist, have close, regular customer contact. They are in an excellent position to spot needs and suggest products. However, they are often handicapped by lack of product knowledge, so they miss opportunities. So, all employees should receive product and sales training and they should be recognized and rewarded for their sales efforts.

■ *Use modern sales tools.* Two important methods for increasing sales efficiently are telemarketing and direct mail. The two have many similarities, even if the technology is different. But, the results favor telemarketing, even though the cost is higher.

Response levels improve when telemarketing and direct mail are combined with special offers, such as:

● Free trial.

● Money-back guarantee.

● Free gift.

● Sweepstakes or contest.

■ *Use trade shows.* Trade shows are a growing sales opportunity. They reduce both selling and purchasing costs by allowing buyers and sellers to have many more contacts in a very short time. These shows can produce immediate sales, although they aren't intended for that purpose. They're designed to facilitate contacts that will be followed up after the show.

CONCLUSION

Marketing is the business function that identifies unfulfilled needs and wants, defines and measures their magnitudes, determines which target markets the company can best serve, decides on appropriate products, services, and programs to serve these markets. In the end, the companies that best satisfy their customers will be winners.

Chapter 4
Purchasing a Business

INTRODUCTION

The title of this book, and much of its content, implies that the main way to get into business is to start from scratch. If marketing a unique skill or product is the reason for going into business, there may not be any alternative to starting a new company. Sometimes, though, the reasons for going into business have more to do with being independent or having more control over daily activities. In that case, the alternative, purchasing an on-going business is very attractive, because it reduces some of the risk of failure.

ORGANIZATION OF CHAPTER

Deciding whether to buy or start-up
How to buy a business
How to buy a franchise

DECIDING WHETHER TO BUY OR START-UP

Many business owners choose to get into business for themselves by purchasing an on going business. Because there is an active market for companies for sale, they find plenty of companies to choose among. And, if they shop carefully, they are better off than if they started new companies.

There are five main advantages of purchasing someone's company:

- *Cost savings.* The business owner who starts up a new business has to pay all the costs of getting into business including advertising, training employees, developing suppliers, experimenting with product lines, design, decorating and signs. By far the biggest cost is the many mistakes an owner makes during start-up. The owner who buys a going business doesn't normally have to incur any of these expenses.

- *Become profitable faster.* A start-up can take from six months to several years before it starts producing profits. By purchasing a profitable operation, the purchaser starts off in a profitable position.

■ *Better chances of success.* Unless the success of a business is totally dependent upon the personality or skill of the former owner, a going business should continue to prosper. Because there is a less risk, lenders will be more willing to finance the purchase of a going business.

■ *Seller training.* Normally, the seller is required to stay on for a while to make the transition easier for customers and to train the new owner. This reduces the amount of previous experience the new owner needs to have.

■ *Reduce competition.* If an owner starts up a new business, and there are similar businesses in the area, competition becomes more fierce. If, instead, the owner buys one of the competitors, competition remains unchanged.

Of course, there are a few negative aspects to buying a business, too.

■ *Higher cost.* The initial cost may be a lot higher than starting a new business. Somebody else has taken a lot of the risk and spent years building a business; the former owner will want to be compensated for both the risk-taking and the time spent. Also, when owners decide to sell the business they have built, they tend to overestimate its value.

■ *Business may not be suitable.* Many business purchasers find the operation is very different from what they expected. They end up undoing the previous owner's operating methods, products or other factors. To avoid this, prospective owners should spend time at the company, even working there, before making a final purchase.

■ *May not be able to manage like the previous owner.* Small companies reflect their owners' management styles and skills. After running their companies for many years, owners make it look easy. A new owner just might not have the necessary skills to handle the old owner's job.

■ *Need higher profits to justify cost of purchase.* When a company is sold to new owners, they take on debt or reduce their savings to pay for it. The cost of this debt reduces the company's profits until it is paid off, often taking as many as five to seven years.

■ *Business may have been misrepresented.* This is one of the biggest, and most common, risks of buying a business. Sometimes the owner of a failing business alters the records in order to make it look more attractive to a potential buyer. Or, the owner makes a profitable company look even more profitable. To guard against this, all buyers must make exhaustive studies of companies they plan to buy.

The decision to buy a business rather than start from scratch brings up another important decision: what form the purchase will take. Many purchasers think only of buying an entire operating business. That thinking limits their options. There really are four main alternatives:

■ Outright purchase of a going business.

■ Outright purchase of a failed business.

■ Purchasing part of a business.

■ Purchasing a franchise.

One overlooked alternative is that of buying just *part* of the assets of a company. Finding a company for sale, a buyer is free to make an offer to buy only part of it: one store of a group, one product line that is unrelated to the rest of the company or the distribution operations of a company that both manufactures and distributes products. Even if a company isn't for sale, the owners may be willing to sell off part of it. There's never any harm in asking.

HOW TO BUY A BUSINESS

The first step to take in buying a business is to *find* one. This means extensive prospecting through many sources, just to find something for sale. There are many sources of information about businesses for sale:

■ *Newspaper business opportunity section.* The local Sunday newspaper or the Friday edition of the *Wall Street Journal* are excellent sources. So are specialized newspapers such as *The Business Opportunity Journal*. The local library can point out others.

- *Trade magazines.* There is a trade association, usually at both the state and national level, for almost every industry. These associations usually publish magazines and newsletters to communicate with their members. The classified advertisements of these publications are a good source of information about companies that are for sale.

- *Business brokers.* Brokers normally work for business owners on a commission basis to sell businesses. But, brokers also are willing to search for businesses that are for sale. For a list of those who belong to the International Association of Business Brokers, call (617) 369-5254.

- *Networking.* Suppliers, vendors, distributors and trade associations are all excellent sources of information for industry-specific businesses as are customers and competitors. One strategy is to ask the owner of a business if it is for sale. Even if the answer is "no," the owner may be able to suggest a company that *is* for sale.

- *CPAs and attorneys.* These business professionals often know of businesses for sale. So do insurance agents, real estate brokers and venture capitalists. Banks can also be a good source; one bank that publishes a newsletter is the First National Bank of Maryland: (800) 842-BANK. Ask local banks if they have listings of businesses for sale.

Investigating a Business

When the search has narrowed down to one or more potential prospects, it's important to make a *thorough* investigation. Some experts say that buyers should expect to spend at least a year finding a business, evaluating its potential and analyzing its marketplace. That's a long time in most situations, but the point these experts make is that the investigation process isn't a quick task. A *quickie* checkup is destined to result in a bad purchase.

Using a Checklist

The checklist in Appendix X is one useful tool for this analysis. The extent of the checklist should suggest how thorough the investigation has to be. Professional help from a CPA and a lawyer may be necessary, too. The CPA is a good resource for investigating the financial and operating health of a business, the lawyer can help examine the legal risks associated with a particular business.

Part of this review is to look at internal documents that show the company's health and past performance. The seller should be willing to talk to the buyer's representative, to provide back tax returns and financial statements, and to permit complete access to all business records. If the seller is not willing to cooperate with a thorough investigation of the financial history and condition of the business, the buyer must BEWARE. Besides internal records, buyers need to talk to customers, the company's landlord, major suppliers or municipal officials. It's a good idea to do a credit check, too.

Finding Out Why the Seller Wants to Sell

An important part of evaluating a business is to learn the *real* reason the owner wants to sell. This is hard to do sometimes, because owners aren't forthright about their reasons. It's essential to find out the real reason, because it could affect whether the company is a good buy. It also helps to know the reason because it could affect the structure of an offer. For example, an owner who wants to retire may entertain an offer that includes a retirement income factor. Or, an owner who is getting out because of overwork or burnout may welcome an opportunity to sell part of the company now, remain for a few years, and then sell the rest. Some of the common reasons for selling a business include:

- Retirement.

- Burnout.

- Escape debts.

- Dump losing business.

- Need money for personal expenses.

- No longer capable of managing.

- Need money for expansion.

- Interested in a different business or career change.

- Poor health.

- Change in marital status.

- Need to move to a different area.

It's a good idea to be suspicious about an owner's motives for selling. When the owner gives an explanation, be sure to ask follow-up questions to verify the explanation. The goal is to search for hidden hazards.

EXAMPLE

A business owner claims to be selling a company and planning to retire. That may be true. Or, the company might be in trouble, it might be running out of cash or a competitor might be planning to open a store down the street. The follow-up questions should confirm the owner's plans. The questions should be conversational:

- "Where are you retiring to?"

- "How are you going to spend retirement?"

- "Was the business able to provide you the funds for retirement?"

The list below contains examples of hidden hazards to look for. Experience shows that business owners either conceal or downplay these factors when they sell their companies.

■ Customer base - will changes over which you have no control impact it?

■ Employees - will they remain? Do you want them to?

■ Supply sources. Will they continue?

■ Possible competition - is a new super store about to break ground? Are there already too many competitors in the market?

■ Possible industry change.

■ Environmental regulations and compliance. Is there contamination on the company's property?

■ Zoning regulations. Are they about to change?

■ Landlord - who owns the property? Will the present terms be continued? Will you be locked into staying?

Negotiating the Purchase

When the number of possibilities is narrowed to one or two, the next step is to negotiate the purchase. The offer should be in writing, should allow time for a more detailed study of the business and provide for cancellation if the business is not right for any reason. Many experienced CPAs and attorneys have developed standard offer forms for this purpose and they should be consulted prior to taking action. The offer should always include a deposit; the deposit shows that the buyer is serious and it can sometimes prevent the seller from entertaining other offers.

Settling on a Price

One problem which buyers typically encounter is the seller who holds out for an unrealistic price. This happens when the seller has been given an unrealistic value by a business broker or when the seller isn't able to look objectively at the company. If the buyer and seller are having trouble coming to terms, one solution is to meet the seller's asking price but get the seller to improve the terms or include other things in the sale. Examples of such seller enhancements are:

- Seller to finance the purchase.

- Seller to work in the company for up to a year.

- Seller to guarantee the company's profit for a year.

- Seller to include assets that weren't originally included in the sale.

Letter of Intent

Once the buyer and the seller have agreed on a preliminary purchase price, they should write a letter of intent to get the owner to take the business off the market. The letter of intent spells out the terms of the sale. A letter of intent is essentially an agreement to write an agreement. It lists the major points of agreement, and is used by the lawyers as the basis of the final agreement. Without a letter of intent, the deal remains unsettled until the final purchase contract is signed. After the letter of intent is signed, the buyer should seek professional help to investigate tax issues and to decide on the form of business and many other issues.

When both parties are ready to complete the sale, the final purchase agreement should be drawn up by an attorney. The attorney should also provide advice about other necessary documents and agreements. Most purchase agreements include some form of a *covenant not to compete* where the former owner agrees not to compete with the buyer for some period of time or within some physical distance. The agreement should also include an indemnification provision where the owner will be responsible for "hidden" liabilities such as environmental contamination. An accountant will help allocate the purchase price into its various components (real estate, if any, fixed assets, and intangibles) as required by the Internal Revenue Service.

HOW TO BUY A FRANCHISE

In many fields, there is yet another way to get into business. Instead of buying a business and operating it independently, some people prefer to operate within a franchise chain. Franchises provide the wisdom, experience and on going business of a corporate parent while providing local business operations the freedom of independent operations. A franchise is a unique partnership between the franchise company and its local outlets. Every chain structures its franchise differently from other chains. Some franchise sellers called franchisors, like McDonalds® and Burger King®, have prospered and, at the same time, made their franchise holders (called a franchisee) wealthy.

How Franchises Operate

Franchise operations are almost always retail operations involving product or service sales. A few involve business-to-business sales.

There are hundreds of different fields available; the list in Figure 4-1 on Page 4-11 is just a sample. One reason to buy a franchise is the industry's track record for success. According to a 1992 survey, nearly 97% of franchisee-owned businesses that opened in the previous five years were still in operation and nearly 86% were owned by the original franchisee. They are definitely worth a careful look.

In a franchise agreement, the business owner and the franchise company make mutual business commitments. The buyer purchases a franchise and enters into a franchise agreement with the franchisor which defines rights and obligations, for example:

- Purchase of supplies from franchisor company.
- Pay a monthly franchise fee, usually a percent of sales.
- Use the franchisor's name and logo in advertising.
- Receive local and national advertising support.
- Meet the franchisor's quality standards.
- Receive a protected territory.
- Receive training and management support.
- Purchase start-up inventory.
- Make a required contribution to an advertising fund.
- Make regular operational and financial reports to the franchise company.

How to Find a Franchise

In addition to the methods described above for finding other businesses for sale, there are four others for potential franchise owners:

- Networking with successful franchise owners.
- Franchise fairs.
- Entrepreneurial magazine ads.
- Consultants and sales agents.

Whenever a seller offers a franchise, the Federal Trade Commission requires it to furnish the buyer an *offering statement*, a document which discloses the risk factors of the franchise. A buyer should ask for this document, read it and have a CPA and lawyer review it, too.

Franchise Cost Considerations

A franchise operator has to pay many of the same start-up costs as for any other start-up business. In addition, the owner has to pay other costs:

- A franchise fee, which ranges from hundreds to thousands of dollars.
- Advertising costs, including signs and logos, required by the franchisor.
- Training programs required by the franchisor.

Owning a franchise means giving up some of the autonomy that is cherished by most small business operators. Most franchisors insist that their franchisees follow their programs rigidly. Even brokers offering franchises for sale advise, "If you can't follow somebody else, don't buy a franchise because your life will be miserable and the franchisor's life will be miserable."

CONCLUSION

By purchasing a going business or a franchise, an owner reduces the risks associated with a business start-up, may increase the likelihood of it becoming profitable faster and reduces the amount of experience needed to go into business. But, buying a business means paying a premium to the person who started the business. The premium may be worth paying, provided it is a reasonable one.

The most important aspect of buying a business, and the one most often overlooked, is that of making a thorough investigation of the company being acquired. This takes time and costs money, but the effort should pay off in reduced risk.

figure 4-1

Examples of franchise opportunities

Airport parking	Home appraisal
Auto service and repair	Home remodeling
Auto sales	Home evaluation
Bakeries	House cleaning services
Beverage sales	Ice cream sales
Bookkeeping services	Limousine service
Bookkeeping systems	Mail forwarding
Building materials sales	Mechanics tool sales
Carpet cleaning	Medical appliances
Cleaning	Motels and hotels
Computer graphics	Nail care
Computer sales	Paging and message services
Computerized bookkeeping	Payroll preparation
Convenience store sales	Pet sales
Copying	Pet grooming
Cosmetics sales	Photo finishing
Dance studio	Printing
Day care	Real estate
Dog walking	Restaurants
Drug store sales	Retail sales
Electronics parts sales	Security alarm monitoring
Employment agencies	Tax preparation
Eyeglass sales	Telephone answering
Financial products sales	Training, languages
Gasoline sales	Training, computer
Gyms	Training, accounting
Hair cutting and styling	Video rentals
Health clubs	

Chapter 5
Small Business Legal Organization

INTRODUCTION

One of the first decisions an owner makes is to choose the type of organization for the business. This choice must be carefully planned because the initial choice is sometimes hard to change. Even changing the company name to add or drop the word "Incorporated," involves added printing cost. In some cases, companies lose the benefit of tax write-offs when changing business form. And, it may take the help of a CPA or lawyer to make the change. So, a poor decision about the type of business organization can cost the company money in administration, income taxes and professional fees.

This chapter discusses the considerations in selecting the right legal organization for a company. It covers the pros and cons of five main forms: Sole Proprietorship, Partnership, Limited Liability Company, "C" Corporation, and "S" Corporation. The business form decision affects the way the company is owned, the way ownership is transferred, the form of the company name, legal protection and income tax payments. The chapter also explains the mechanics of setting up a company, including deciding on accounting periods and accounting methods, registering with Federal and State agencies and getting licenses to do business. The companion checklist to this chapter is in Appendix A.

ORGANIZATION OF THIS CHAPTER

Types of business organization
Sole proprietorship
Partnership
Limited Liability Company
"C" corporation
"S" corporation
Setting up a company in Connecticut
Forming a corporation, LLC or partnership
Applying for tax numbers
Getting permission to do business
Insurance policies

TYPES OF BUSINESS ORGANIZATION

Every company has to select a form of organization. The different types, together with their rights and protection, are defined by Connecticut statute. The way a company pays income taxes is defined by the Internal Revenue Code and Connecticut Statutes. Within limits, a company is allowed to change its type of organization at any time. There are five main types of business organization:

- Sole Proprietorship.
- Partnership.
- Limited Liability Company.
- "C" Corporation.
- "S" Corporation.

This section is an overview of the five main organization types. The text continues with a detailed description of each organization type. Figure 5-1 on Page 5-3 summarizes the differences among the types.

Sole Proprietorship

A Sole Proprietorship is the simplest form of business. It is owned and operated by one person. A Sole Proprietorship does not involve creating a new legal entity or transferring assets. Rather, the owner simply segregates a group of assets and dedicates them to the business. All of the taxes of the business are paid by the owner. The owner has unlimited personal liability for the debts of the business.

Partnership

A Partnership is generally the simplest way to do business when there is more than one owner. The Partnership is a separate legal entity. Each partner contributes money, skills, labor, property and/or other capital to the partnership and shares in the profits and losses. Every partner is an agent of the partnership and can take actions that obligate the partnership and the other partners. Partners, like Sole Proprietors, are responsible for their shares of the company's taxes and have unlimited personal liability for business debts.

One form of Partnership, the Limited Partnership, allows some partners to limit their liabilities to the amount of their capital contribution to the Partnership. This form of partnership is not common for small businesses, but may apply in some cases.

figure 5-1

Comparison of different business forms

	Sole Prop	Partnership	LLC	"C" Corp	"S" Corp
Separate legal entity		Normally	✓	✓	✓
Free transferability of ownership		✓	✓	✓	✓
Limits owners' legal liability			✓	✓	✓
Income taxed at owner level	✓	✓	✓		Federal only
Income taxed at business level				✓	
Generally must use calendar year	✓	✓	✓		✓
Owners take income out as salary				✓	✓
Owners take income out as "draw"	✓	✓	✓		
Loss deductible from owners' other income	✓	✓	✓		✓
Can write-off owners' health insurance				✓	✓
Owners pay self employment tax on income	✓	✓	✓		
Must register with Secretary of State			✓	✓	✓
Tax return filed	Sched "C"	Form 1065	Form 1065	Form 1120	Form 1120S
Double taxation of dividends				✓	
Can exclude part of dividend income from tax				✓	

Limited Liability Company

A Limited Liability Company (LLC) is the newest form of legal entity permitted to do business in Connecticut. An LLC is a hybrid entity that combines a partnership's tax advantages and the corporate benefit of limited liability for its owners. The LLC is a separate legal entity with at least two "members." Each member contributes money, skills, labor or other assets to the LLC and shares in the profits. Every member of the LLC can take actions to obligate the LLC.

"C" Corporation

There are two types of Corporation, "C" and "S". Both are types of businesses wherein shareholders form a separate legal entity. The difference between the types lies in the way they are taxed, and the name comes from the section of the Internal Revenue Code that defines how they are taxed. Shareholders of both types of Corporation have the advantage of limiting their personal liability for business obligations.

A "C" Corporation pays federal and state income taxes on its earnings. When the earnings are distributed to the "C" Corporation's shareholders as dividends, they are taxed again. This double taxation is one of the big drawbacks of the "C" corporation.

"S" Corporation

An "S" Corporation has the same legal attributes as a "C" Corporation. However, an "S" Corporation generally does not have to pay federal income taxes; its shareholders pay taxes on their share of income on their personal tax returns. This allows it to escape the double taxation of a "C" Corporation and to enjoy the lower tax rates of individual taxpayers. Connecticut charges "S" Corporations the same taxes as it does "C" Corporations.

SOLE PROPRIETORSHIP

Being one's own boss has its advantages and disadvantages. Sole Proprietors are free to make their own decisions and engage in business wherever and whenever they want. The only restrictions placed on the Sole Proprietor's operational flexibility are licensing and fictitious name statutes.

Legal Considerations for Sole Proprietorships

Personal Liability

A Sole Proprietor has unlimited personal liability for the obligations of the business. The Sole Proprietor's liability for business debts can exceed the amount of capital actually contributed to the business. Both the personal and business assets of the Sole Proprietor are subject to the claims of all creditors, both business and personal.

Separate Legal Entity

A Sole Proprietorship is not a distinct legal entity apart from the Sole Proprietor. Even if a Sole Proprietorship operates under an assumed or fictitious name, the name has no bearing on the legal treatment of the Sole Proprietor.

Management and Control

The Sole Proprietor is free to make business decisions and to engage in any legal business with very few state licensing or registration requirements.

Continuity of Existence

Unlike the other forms of business organization, the Sole Proprietorship ends with the death of the Sole Proprietor. Many business rights, such as franchises and licenses also terminate on the death of a Sole Proprietor, and cannot be transferred to the Proprietor's heirs, unless the documents that created the rights allow them to pass to the Proprietor's heirs at death. In such cases, it may be a good idea to choose a different form of business organization with continuity of existence.

Transferability of Interests

A Sole Proprietor has complete freedom to sell or transfer any portion of the Sole Proprietorship. The only restrictions on a Sole Proprietor may be in the form of franchise or license restrictions on transferability of business assets.

Expense and Formality of Organization

A Sole Proprietorship can be formed without any required filing or documentation. However, if a Sole Proprietor chooses to use a fictitious name, an inexpensive Trade Name Certificate must be prepared and filed with the local town clerk's office.

Sources of Operating Capital

A Sole Proprietorship is generally funded from the individual assets of the Sole Proprietor and third party loans. A Sole Proprietor may grant security interests and mortgage interests in personal assets as collateral to third party creditors.

Tax Considerations for Sole Proprietorships

Formation of Business Organization

There are generally no income tax consequences when a Sole Proprietorship is formed. A Sole Proprietor, however, should keep separate records for business and personal finances.

Income Taxes

A Sole Proprietorship is not a separate taxpayer. All the taxes of the Sole Proprietorship are paid by the Sole Proprietor. A Sole Proprietorship reports its business profits on a Schedule C, which is part of the Proprietor's Form 1040.

For Social Security or FICA purposes, the income of a Sole Proprietorship is considered to be the Sole Proprietor's "salary". The proprietor pays self-employment tax on this income, in lieu of the FICA tax paid by an employer or employee. The self-employment tax is figured on Schedule SE, which is also part of the Sole Proprietor's Form 1040.

Deductibility of Losses

A Sole Proprietor may generally offset proprietorship losses against other personal income. However, the deduction for losses may be limited by Internal Revenue Service rules. One possible limitation for a Sole Proprietorship is the "hobby loss" rule. The Internal Revenue Service may disallow losses from activities considered to be hobbies rather than profit-making endeavors. Internal

Revenue Service rules presume that an activity is not a hobby if it makes a profit for three out of five years. A Proprietor who experiences losses upon starting up a business can avoid hobby loss problems for the first four years by filing Internal Revenue Service Form 5213.

Even if a Sole Proprietor's business loses money for three or more years, an argument can still be made that the business was engaged in for profit. The extent of time and effort devoted to the operation of the Sole Proprietorship, the manner in which it is conducted, the expertise of the Sole Proprietor, and the nature of the business activity are all factors which can be considered.

Choice of Tax Year

A Sole Proprietorship must have the same tax year as the Sole Proprietor, which is generally the calendar year.

Sale of an Interest

The sale of an interest in a Sole Proprietorship has distinct tax consequences because a Sole Proprietorship is not considered a separate legal entity. Therefore, gain or loss on a sale is not measured by gain or loss on an interest in an entity, but rather upon the gain or loss on the sale of each individual asset. This results in gain being allocated between "ordinary income" and "capital gain" type items.

Conclusion - Sole Proprietorships

A Sole Proprietorship is indeed the simplest form in which to do business. But, that doesn't mean it is the right form of business for all small businesses. The next few sections of this chapter examine alternative forms of business. Business owners must consider the pros and cons of each before making a final selection.

PARTNERSHIP

One of the most important aspects of a Partnership is the Partnership agreement, which defines Partners' rights and obligations. Personal conflicts between Partners can cause problems, which can result in dissolution. An individual, a corporation, a trust, an estate, and even another partnership may be a Partner in a Partnership.

Legal Considerations for Partnerships

Personal Liability

A Partner in a Partnership has unlimited personal liability for the obligations of the Partnership. This includes liability for actions taken by the other partners when they are acting in the name of the Partnership.

Separate Legal Entity

In Connecticut, Partnerships are separate legal entities. Partnerships can own property in their own names. They can sue and be sued.

Management and Control

A Partnership is similar to a Sole Proprietorship in that there are few formal restrictions on the management of a Partnership. Unless otherwise provided in a written Partnership agreement, the business affairs of a Partnership are governed by the vote of a majority of the voting Partners.

Continuity of Existence

A Partnership has limited continuity of existence. Upon the death of a Partner, a Partnership dissolves under state law, which does not necessarily cause a dissolution for federal income tax purposes. A dissolved Partnership does not necessarily liquidate and distribute its assets. It can form into a new Partnership under state law and continue the business operations of the former dissolved Partnership.

Transferability of Interests

Partners may not transfer their interests in a Partnership without the consent of the other Partners, unless the written Partnership agreement allows them to. They are allowed to pledge their interests to secure loans. It is wise to word the Partnership agreement so as to prevent Partners from pledging their Partnership interests without the consent of the other Partners.

Expense and Formality of Organization

A Partnership can usually be formed with little expense or formality. *However, it is very important for the Partners to have a formal Partnership agreement.* In the absence of a written agreement, the Connecticut Uniform Partnership Act determines the rights and obligations of the Partners.

Sources of Operating Capital

A Partnership has more flexibility than a Sole Proprietorship in obtaining operating capital. Besides capital contributions from its Partners, a Partnership can use Partner loans and third party loans as a source of operating capital. With the consent of the Partners, a Partnership can also sell more interests in the Partnership to raise operating capital.

Tax Considerations for Partnerships

Formation of Business Organization

A Partnership is formed when partners contribute money, property or services to the Partnership and begin to do business. Sometimes, the form of this contribution can result in taxes to the partners. The two ways to form are the taxable formation and the nontaxable formation.

- *Nontaxable Formation.* This is the normal method. The Partnership is formed without any tax consequences when property is contributed to a Partnership in exchange for an interest in the Partnership.

- *Taxable Formation.* This can happen in some situations. One is where a Partner receives a Partnership interest in return for services performed. The Partner receives taxable income and the Partnership receives a tax deduction for the value of the transfer. The other situation is where a Partner transfers property that has a mortgage. If the Partnership assumes the mortgage, the transferring Partner may have taxable income. The taxable amount will depend upon many factors, including the Partner's tax basis in the property contributed and the amount of the mortgage assumed by the Partnership.

Income Taxes

A Partnership is similar to a Sole Proprietorship in that it does not pay taxes directly either to the Internal Revenue Service or to Connecticut. Income, losses, some deductions and credits pass directly to the Partners and are reported on their individual income tax returns. These "pass through" items are taxed as if the individual Partners had earned them directly.

A Partnership files a separate Partnership Return of Income every year. This is an information report, however, and no tax is due with it. Included in the return are Schedules K-1 for the Partners, which they use in preparing their personal tax returns. Thus, each Partners' income is taxed at individual tax rates.

The allocation of Partnership income depends on the Partnership agreement. It can be simple or very complicated. If there are changes in ownership percentages during a tax year, they will affect the income allocation.

For social security tax purposes, none of the income generated by a Partnership is subject to withholding. This is also true for other compensation, such as guaranteed payments, the Partnership may pay the partners. Instead, the partners are responsible for their own taxes. Instead of FICA tax, they pay a self-employment tax, which is figured on the partners' Form 1040 Schedule SE. Instead of withholding for income taxes, they make quarterly tax deposits.

Deductibility of Losses

Partners may use Partnership losses against their other income. There are several limitations on the use of these losses, however, and a Partner who receives a K-1 form showing a loss should seek professional advice.

Choice of Tax Year

A Partnership must adopt the same tax year as the Partners owning a majority interest in the Partnership's profits and capital. Therefore, if a Partnership consists of individual taxpayers, the Partnership has to use the calendar year.

Sale of an Interest

The sale or exchange of a Partnership interest generally results in capital gain or loss to the selling Partner. If a cash basis Partnership has "unrealized receivables" or "substantially appreciated" inventory items, a portion of the gain or loss on the sale or exchange by a Partner is considered ordinary income.

Liquidation or Dissolution

If a Partnership is dissolved or liquidated, Partners get their interests back, either in cash or property. A partner's interest is normally not taxed, because it has already been taxed. Partners recognize taxable income only if the cash distributed in liquidation exceeds the adjusted basis of the Partnership interest of the Partner immediately before the distribution.

Conclusion - Partnerships

Partners have a great deal of freedom in the Partnership form of business organization. Of course, that small step above the Sole Proprietorship form brings a big increase in complexity over the Sole Proprietorship.

LIMITED LIABILITY COMPANY

The Limited Liability Company (LLC) form of business organization provides protection from personal liability for its owners, who are known as *members*. The LLC can offer this protection and also provide the tax advantages of a partnership. The operations of a LLC are usually governed by a written operating agreement, or in absence of one, by the Connecticut Limited Liability Company Act.

Legal Considerations for LLCs

Personal Liability

A member in a LLC is not liable for the debts and liabilities of the LLC, unless the member expressly guarantees them. Like a corporation, this protection will depend on the members conforming to the statutory requirements for limited liability companies.

Separate Legal Entity

A LLC is a separate legal entity that may own property in its own name and may sue and be sued.

Management and Control

Management and control of a LLC is normally delegated, through its articles of organization, to its Manager. The Manager is elected by the members, but doesn't have to be a member. The Manager also doesn't have to be an individual; another company can be appointed as Manager. So, the Manager of an LLC can be another LLC, a corporation or a partnership. If the members do not choose to appoint a Manager, the LLC is governed by the vote of the majority of the Members.

Continuity of Existence

A LLC has limited continuity of existence. While its articles of organization must state the latest date upon which the LLC is to dissolve, its articles of organization may be amended at any time to extend this period of time.

Transferability of interests

A member's interest in a LLC is personal property and can be sold or transferred in whole or in part, unless the operating agreement forbids transfers. The sale of an interest does not dissolve the LLC or entitle the purchaser to participate in the management of the LLC, or exercise any rights of a member. However, a purchaser may become a member if:

■ The seller gives the purchaser that right, or

■ At least a majority of the members consent.

Expense and Formality of Organization

A LLC has a number of formal requirements before coming into existence. Included among them is the filing of articles of organization. Similar to articles of incorporation, the LLC's articles of organization must include certain general information, such as its name and address; the latest date it is to dissolve; if management is to be vested in a Manager or Managers; and the nature of the business to be transacted. This final requirement could be a simple statement that the LLC will engage in any lawful activity. The LLC must also file with the Secretary of State a written statement, which sets forth its name and the name of a statutory agent for service process, as well as the agent's address.

The LLC must also keep at its office: a current and past list of the name and address of each member and Manager; the articles of organization and any operating agreement; a statement regarding the agreed value of property or services contributed by each member, including cash; a statement concerning the events on which the LLC will be dissolved; and any other documents that are part of the operating agreement.

Sources of Operating Capital

A LLC may obtain operating capital from member contributions and loans. With the consent of the members, the LLC may also sell more interests in the LLC to raise operating capital.

Tax Considerations for LLCs

Formation of Business Organization

A LLC is formed when members contribute money, property or services to the LLC, file the required documents with the Secretary of State and begin to do business. As with the Partnership, the form of this contribution can result in taxes to the members:

■ *Nontaxable Formation.* This is the normal method. The LLC is formed without any tax consequences when property is contributed to it in exchange for an interest in the LLC.

■ *Taxable Formation.* This can happen in some situations. Like a partnership and corporation, this will happen when a member receives a LLC interest in return for services performed. The member receives taxable income and the LLC receives a tax deduction for the value of the transfer. The other situation is where a member transfers property that is subject to a liability. If the LLC assumes the liability, the member may have taxable income. The taxable amount will depend upon many factors, including the member's tax basis in the property contributed and the amount of the liability assumed by the LLC.

Income Taxes

If structured properly, a LLC is like a partnership in that it does not pay taxes directly either to the Internal Revenue Service or to Connecticut. Income, losses, some deductions and credits pass directly to the members and are reported on their individual income tax returns. These "pass through" items are taxed as if the individual members had earned them directly.

A LLC files a separate Return of Income (Form 1065) every year. This is an information report, however, and no tax is due with it. Included in the return will be Schedules K-1 for the members, which they use in preparing their personal tax returns. Thus, each member's income is taxed at individual tax rates.

The allocation of the income of the LLC depends on the operating agreement. It can be simple or very complicated. If there are changes in ownership percentages during a tax year, they will affect the income allocation.

Like a partnership, for social security tax purposes, the income generated by a LLC is considered to be each member's "salary." This is in addition to any other compensation the LLC may pay the member. The member pays self-employment tax on this income as well as on any other compensation, since there is no FICA being paid. The self-employment tax is figured on the member's Form 1040 Schedule SE.

Deductibility of Losses

A member may use LLC losses against their other income. There are several limitations on the use of these losses, however, and a member who receives a K-1 form showing a loss should seek professional advice.

Choice of Tax Year

Like a partnership, a LLC must adopt the same tax year as the members owning a majority interest in the LLC's profits and capital. Therefore, if a LLC has individual members, the LLC has to use the calendar year.

Sale of an Interest

The sale or exchange of a LLC interest generally results in capital gain or loss to the selling member. Like a partnership, if a cash basis LLC has "unrealized receivables" or "substantially appreciated" inventory items, a portion of the gain or loss on the sale or exchange by a member is considered ordinary income.

Liquidation or Dissolution

If a LLC is dissolved or liquidated, members get their interests back either in cash or property. A member's interest is normally not taxed, because it has already been taxed. Members recognize taxable income only if the cash distributed in liquidation exceeds the adjusted basis of the LLC interest of the member immediately before the distribution.

Conclusion - LLCs

New businesses and businesses currently operating in the Corporate or Partnership form should evaluate the costs and potential benefits of conversion to a LLC. Generally, limited and general Partnerships may make the conversion without paying any taxes. Corporations (including S corporations) will ordinarily incur tax costs that may outweigh the benefits of conversion.

Questions remain about the scope of limited liability protection for members of limited liability companies operating in states that have not enacted LLC legislation. As more states enact this legislation, however, it is possible that the LLC will become the preferred form of business entity for small businesses.

"C" CORPORATION

The Corporate form of business organization provides the most protection from personal liability for its owners, the Shareholders. Corporations can give their employees such fringe benefits as stock options, pensions and group insurance more effectively than other types of business can. However, these advantages are paid for with a "double-tax" on Corporate profits. Before choosing the corporate form of business, business owners must carefully weigh the pros and cons. The "C" Corporation is one of two types of corporation. The legal characteristics of both types are identical; the tax characteristics are different.

Legal Considerations for "C" Corporations

Limited Liability

The Limited liability available to Corporate Shareholders is one of the major non-tax advantages in the Corporate form of business organization. Corporate Shareholders are not liable for the debts and liabilities of the Corporation, unless they expressly guarantee them. This protection depends on the shareholders conforming to the statutory requirements for Corporations. If they do not, creditors may be able to sue the shareholders directly, "piercing the corporate veil". This can easily happen to small, closely held family businesses which overlook the formalities of Corporate existence.

Separate Legal Entity

A Corporation is a separate legal entity that may own property in its own name and may sue and be sued.

Management and Control

Management and control of a Corporation is centralized in its Board of Directors. The Directors are elected by the Shareholders. In Connecticut, Boards of Directors must have at least three members, unless there are fewer than three shareholders; in that case, the number of board members must be at least as many as the number of Shareholders. In a small business, the sole Shareholder is also the sole Director and President of the Corporation. That Shareholder must remember that the responsibilities of a Shareholder, Director and Officer are different. In Connecticut, there must be a President and a Secretary of the Corporation even if there is only one shareholder.

Continuity of Existence

A Corporation under Connecticut law has perpetual existence unless its Certificate of Incorporation specifies a limited life. This means that the death of a Shareholder, even a sole Shareholder, does not end the Corporation's existence. If the Corporation fails to file the required biennial reports with the Secretary of State, it can be dissolved by the state.

Transferability of Interests

Shares of a Corporation are easier to transfer than any other business interests. Shareholders are free to sell any and all portions of their shares. The Shareholders of a closely held Corporation should have a written Shareholder's agreement that restricts the transfer of stock by the Shareholders. The purpose of such an agreement is to prevent a Shareholder from being forced to contend with an unwanted new fellow Shareholder. Typically, a Shareholder in a closely held corporation must first offer to sell to fellow Shareholders or to the company before selling to outsiders.

Expense and Formality of Organization

A Corporation has a number of formal requirements before coming into legal existence. Included among them in Connecticut is to file a Certificate of Incorporation and to appoint an agent (who can be an officer of the company) to receive official legal documents. The newly formed Corporation must then issue stock certificates. The Corporation must pay a fee to the Secretary of State's office to be officially registered. The Corporation's Certificate of Incorporation must include certain information:

- Corporate name.

- Statement of the purposes for which the Corporation is being formed.

- Length of time for which the Corporation is being formed, if not perpetual.

- Maximum amount and type of capital stock to be authorized.

- Initial value of capital stock. This must be at least $1,000.

Sources of Operating Capital

A Corporation is the most flexible form of business organization for obtaining operating capital. Corporations can issue various types of equity instruments such as voting common stock, non-voting common stock and various types of preferred stock. A Corporation also can get operating capital through Shareholder loans and loans from third party creditors.

Tax Considerations for "C" Corporations

Formation of Business Organization

Like Partnerships, Corporations may be organized in either nontaxable or taxable transactions:

■   *Nontaxable Incorporation.* Normally, there is no tax on property transferred to a Corporation by a Shareholder in exchange for stock in the Corporation.

■   *Taxable Incorporation.* There may be a tax payable if a Shareholder transfers property subject to liabilities. If the Corporation assumes the debt, the Shareholder may have to pay tax on the built-in profit in the property.

Income Taxes

A "C" Corporation is a separate legal entity and pays its own income taxes. When the "C" Corporation pays a dividend the Shareholders who receive the dividend have to include it on their personal tax return. Thus, there is a double tax on corporate profits, because the dividends are not deductible expenses for a Corporation. A way to avoid the double tax is to pay as much as possible to Shareholders in tax deductible items such as salaries, bonuses, commissions and rental payments. These payments are allowable deductions if they are "ordinary and necessary" business expenses and "reasonable" in amount.

Deductibility of Losses

The Shareholders of a "C" Corporation cannot deduct Corporate losses against their other sources of personal income. The "C" Corporation retains these losses. It can either carry them back and get refunds of previous years' taxes or carry them forward to future tax years to offset future taxable income.

Choice of Tax Year

A "C" Corporation can choose any month as the end of its fiscal year for income tax purposes. However, Corporations that perform personal services may be required to use December 31 as a tax year end.

Sale of an Interest

The Shareholders of a "C" Corporation will generally recognize capital gain or loss on the sale of their stock. When selling shares in a closely-held corporation, shareholders should seek professional guidance **before** the sale for two reasons. One is that capital loss write-offs on personal income tax returns are normally limited to $3,000 per year, while loss write-offs on stock in most small business corporations have a $100,000 per year limit. The other is that the sale of stock in certain Corporations (known as "collapsible" corporations) may result in ordinary gain or loss instead of capital gain or loss. *Beginning in 1993, the IRS allows original investors to exclude up to $50,000 of the gain in eligible small businesses after five years.*

Liquidation or Dissolution

A liquidation and dissolution of a "C" Corporation is a taxable event for both the corporation and its shareholders. The Corporation has a taxable gain or loss on the property it sells or transfers in liquidation. Then, the Shareholders have a taxable gain or loss on the difference between the fair market value of the property they receive in the liquidation and the tax basis of their stock. The combined federal and state taxes on a complete dissolution and liquidation of a "C" Corporation can easily exceed 50%.

Conclusion - "C" Corporation

A "C" Corporation, is a form of business organization that offers many legal and tax advantages to its owners. It can also create some difficult tax problems for its owners. The "S" Corporation, discussed in the next section of this Chapter, eliminates some of those tax problems.

"S" CORPORATION

An "S" Corporation is identical to a "C" Corporation for legal purposes. The main advantage of "S" Corporation status is that it allows its Shareholders most of the tax advantages of a Partnership along with the legal advantages of a "C" Corporation. The "S" Corporation generally eliminates the problem of double taxation usually associated with the "C" Corporation form of business organization, but keeps the corporation's advantage of limited liability.

Legal Considerations for "S" Corporations

In most respects, the legal considerations of an "S" Corporation are like those of a "C" Corporation. The previous section on "C" corporations contains a discussion of the factors. They include:

- Limited Liability.
- Separate Legal Entity.
- Management and Control.
- Continuity of Existence.
- Transferability of Interests.
- Expense and Formality of Organization.

Sources of Operating Capital for an "S" Corporation are similar to those for a "C" Corporation. However, Internal Revenue Service regulations have a significant impact on how Shareholders lend money to their "S" Corporations. If the loans are not properly executed, they could result in a second class of stock which would terminate the "S" corporation status.

Tax Considerations for "S" Corporations

Formation of Business Organization

This is the same as for a "C" Corporation. There are two other factors: Connecticut taxes and the Internal Revenue Service requirements to qualify as an "S" corporation.

Connecticut does not recognize Subchapter "S" Corporations for tax purposes. Therefore, an "S" Corporation is treated like a "C" Corporation for state income tax purposes, except for interest, dividends and other "pass-through" items of income, losses and deductions. These are reported on the shareholders' tax returns rather than the corporation's.

The Internal Revenue Service imposes several requirements on Corporations that seek "S" Corporation status. An "S" corporation must have these characteristics:

- United States Corporation.

- No more than 35 Shareholders.

- Shareholders must be individuals, estates, and certain trusts.

- Nonresident aliens cannot be Shareholders.

- No more than one class of stock.

- Cannot own or be owned by another Corporation.

A corporation becomes an "S" corporation by filing an Internal Revenue Service Form 2553 within 2½ months of the start of any tax year. Once made, the election is effective for that year and until it is revoked.

There are two ways to revoke the "S" Corporation status. One way is for the owners of over half of the stock to elect to revoke it. The other is by not meeting an eligibility requirement. For example, a shareholder could sell one share of stock to a corporation and force the corporation to lose its "S" status. For this reason, the shareholder agreement should prevent shareholders from taking actions that may invalidate the "S" election unless they have permission.

Income Taxes

"S" Corporations are taxed like Partnerships. The corporation files an information return, Form 1120S, but pays no Federal tax on it. Income, losses, deductions, and credits of the "S" Corporation flow into the shareholders' personal income tax returns; they pay income taxes at personal tax rates. Connecticut makes "S" corporations pay the same taxes as "C" corporations, but the shareholders may "back out" those amounts on their Connecticut individual returns.

Deductibility of Losses

If an "S" Corporation loses money, its Shareholders can deduct the losses against their other income. However, their loss deductions are limited to their investment in the corporation.

Choice of Tax Year

"S" Corporations are generally required to use calendar years. If an "S" corporation's shareholders want a different tax year, they may elect to have one.

But, they may have to make advance tax payments to give the Internal Revenue Service the same cash flow as a calendar year.

Sale of an Interest

Taxes on the sale of "S" Corporation stock are the same as for "C" Corporation stock.

Liquidation or Dissolution

When an "S" corporation is liquidated or dissolved, it does not have the same double tax problem as a "C" Corporation. Any gains and losses flow through to the personal tax returns of the Shareholders.

Conclusion - "S" Corporations

The "S" corporation form is the clear favorite for small companies that need the liability protection of a corporation. One main drawback is that the "S" Corporation must have the same tax year as the owners, which rules out selecting a tax year that comes at a convenient time of year. This drawback has not prevented millions of companies from choosing to do business as "S" corporations.

SETTING UP A COMPANY IN CONNECTICUT

After deciding on a business form, the business owner has two other decisions to make and a few actions to take before starting up. Appendix A is a checklist of start-up actions.

Decision: Accounting Periods

Every business must have an "accounting year." This is the annual accounting period the business uses for keeping records, figuring net income and paying income taxes.

There are two alternate accounting periods that any company can use:

■ Calendar year. A year which ends on December 31.

■ Fiscal year. A year which ends any other month.

A business adopts its tax year when it files its first federal income tax return. If it adopts a calendar year, the accounting year ends on December 31. A fiscal year is an accounting year ending on the last day of any month except December. It keeps using the same accounting year unless it elects to change to a different one. A business can use different periods for accounting and taxes. For example, the tax year could end December 31 and the accounting year could end June 30. But, most businesses find it convenient and less expensive to use the same period for both.

Generally, Partnerships, Limited Liability Companies and "S" Corporations are required to use a calendar year as their tax year. Most corporations that provide professional services, such as a law firm, medical practice and dentists, must also use a calendar year. Most Sole Proprietorships also use a calendar year because the owner files tax returns on a calendar year basis. As a result, generally, only businesses operating as "C" Corporations can adopt fiscal years.

Decision: Accounting Method

A business figures its net income under one of two accounting methods:

■ Cash method.

■ Accrual method.

Cash Method

Under the cash method, income includes money that is received and expenses include money that is paid out. "Received," under the cash method, includes money that is available to the business. Thus, a customer check sitting in the company's mailbox is "received," whether or not anyone takes it out.

Likewise, the cash method modifies the term "paid." It does not include expenses that are paid in advance.

Companies that own merchandise or manufacturing inventory cannot use the cash method of accounting; they have to use the accrual method. "C" corporations cannot use the cash method unless their average annual gross receipts are less than $5 million.

Accrual Method

Under the accrual method of accounting, income includes money that has been earned and expenses include those that are incurred. The goal of the accrual method is to match income earned and expenses incurred in the same time period.

Income is earned (and therefore taxable) when the business has a fixed right to receive the income and the amount of the income can be reasonably determined. Income can be earned in one year and received the following year.

Expenses are incurred by a business in the tax year that the business owes the expense and the amount of the expense can be reasonably determined. An expense can be incurred in one year and not actually paid until the following year.

The cash method is normally the one to use in order to reduce taxes. That is because income is usually lower under the cash method than it is under the accrual method.

FORMING A CORPORATION, LLC OR PARTNERSHIP

The earlier sections of this chapter discussed the legal mechanics of forming corporations and partnerships. There are no mechanics at all in forming a sole proprietorship. There are two other actions that may be necessary in forming a corporation or partnership: drafting agreements and registering a fictitious business name.

Shareholder or partner agreement

When a company has more than one owner, even if they are a married couple, they may have a disagreement and want to split apart or, one owner might die, become disabled or go bankrupt. Every business needs an agreement between the owners that avoids having the owners occupied in lawsuits trying to resolve the business' fate. A good shareholder or partner agreement should deal with several possibilities:

■ Death or disability of working owner.

■ Sale of owner's interest.

■ Retirement of owner.

■ Bankruptcy of business.

■ Bankruptcy of owner.

■ Policy disagreement between owners.

Fictitious names

If the company does business using a name other than the company name, or if a sole proprietor does business under a fictitious name, the name should be registered with the local town clerk. Registration protects the company from another business stealing goodwill by using the same name.

APPLYING FOR TAX NUMBERS

Most companies need three different identification numbers:

■ Federal identification number.

■ State unemployment identification number.

■ State tax identification number.

The company's CPA firm, payroll service or lawyer should have the forms to use for applying for these numbers. Companies can also get the forms from Community Accounting and Aid Services, the Connecticut Small Business Development Center, Internal Revenue Service, Connecticut Department of Revenue Services and the State Labor Department.

Federal Identification Numbers

Every Partnership, LLC and Corporation must have a Federal employer identification number (EIN) to use as its taxpayer identification number. A Sole Proprietorship can use the owner's social security number as its taxpayer identification number. However, a sole proprietorship must have an EIN if it:

- Pays wages.

- Files pension or excise tax returns.

The company can get an EIN by filing Internal Revenue Service Form SS-4, Application for Employer Identification Number. The EIN may also be applied for by phone. Appendix I lists the toll-free number to call to get a federal EIN.

Once a company registers for an EIN, the Internal Revenue Service automatically mails the necessary Internal Revenue Service forms: tax deposit coupons, quarterly report forms, income tax forms and tax rate booklets.

State Unemployment Identification Numbers

Any business that has employees must have a Connecticut unemployment identification number and pay state unemployment taxes. The company gets this number by filing Form UC-1A, the application form for a Connecticut unemployment tax registration number. These are issued by the Connecticut Department of Labor, which issues the numbers by mail or telephone. The department's number and address are listed in Appendix I.

State Tax Identification Numbers

A company has to register with the Connecticut Department of Revenue Services if it makes taxable sales, makes taxable purchases or has employees. The company must file Form REG-1, Application for a Tax Registration Number. The registration number costs a small filing fee for most applicants. Connecticut issues the number either by telephone or mail. Appendix I lists the address and toll-free number to call to get a Connecticut tax number.

When it files Form REG-1, the company receives a sales tax permit. The permit lasts for two years and is renewed automatically. The permit must be displayed conspicuously at the place of businesses. A company in a business without a permit will be subject to a fine. The company also receives the necessary report forms and updates on tax regulations.

GETTING PERMISSION TO DO BUSINESS

The state and local governments regulate who can do business and where they can do it. There are two sources for these regulations: town zoning laws and regulations of the state agencies that issue professional licenses.

Zoning laws

The local town zoning board decides what types of business can be operated from a residential area. The home-based business owner should check on regulations before opening for business.

Professional licenses

Most skilled professionals, such as hairdressers and contractors, have to get special licenses before they can sell their services to the public. Appendix P is a current list of the licensed professions and their licensing boards.

INSURANCE POLICIES

The legal organization is just one way to protect a business. The other is with adequate insurance coverage. Appendix A contains a checklist of insurance needs for small businesses.

CONCLUSION

Business organization decisions can affect income taxes, legal protection and continuity of the company. A business owner should consult with accounting and legal professionals before making a final decision. The decision involves balancing tax advantages, administrative costs and legal protection. After making the decision, the owners should form the business and register with tax and regulatory authorities.

INTRODUCTION

Small companies need money to start up, operate and expand. Most of them get started with a small investment of the owners' savings. But, there are many other sources. Despite recent credit shortages, Connecticut has an excellent history of business lending and investment. It still surpasses most other states in start-up capital investments. Recently, state and federal government agencies and banks have made millions of dollars available to small companies that want to expand and hire new employees.

This chapter discusses alternatives and procedures for raising money to start-up or expand a business. It reviews sources of money, the pros and cons of each source and how to get money from each source. It also reviews Federal and Connecticut government programs for small businesses and those owned by women and members of minority groups.

ORGANIZATION OF CHAPTER

Sources of capital ... and risks
Determining how much money is needed
Calculating capital needs
Anticipating needs for more money
Debt versus equity financing
Debt financing
Equity financing
Sources of business capital
How lenders charge for loans
Preparing a proposal for financing
Getting outside help with the financing process
Small Business Administration programs
Financing and management assistance programs
Federal assistance
State assistance
Opportunities for minorities and women

SOURCES OF CAPITAL ... AND RISKS

Starting a business calls for having enough money to operate successfully through the company's formative years. Sources of start-up money include: individual investors, banks, federal, state and local government agencies, venture capitalists, customers and suppliers. The right source of money for a company depends on its situation; no two are exactly alike.

An entrepreneur, according to Webster's is "...one who assumes the risks of business." Entrepreneurs must face one fact: lenders do not want to take on business risks. Therefore, they require collateral from the borrower to protect their loan. Banks, financial institutions and public agencies are required by law to protect their loans with collateral.

DETERMINING HOW MUCH MONEY IS NEEDED

The primary cause of business failure is cash shortages. If a company does not have enough cash to carry it through tough times and keep it operating in periods of expansion, it can fail, even if its sales are expanding rapidly. During an expansion, a company needs money to buy inventory, finance accounts receivable, hire people and expand physical space. This requires more cash than when the company is growing slowly and can be financed from profits.

It is very hard to start a company on a shoestring. If a company estimates its cash needs on the low side, it could be worse off than if it had no cash at all. That is because when it runs out of cash during start-up, it might not be able to get cash to start over. The safe thing to do is raise more capital then needed to meet the company's minimum needs. A good safety margin is 10-20% above estimated needs.

CALCULATING CAPITAL NEEDS

The start-up budget is an essential part of the business plan. Chapter 1, Business Planning, discussed the need for this budget and mentioned some of its components. Appendix K is a worksheet for cash requirements and Appendix L is a worksheet for cash availability. This section shows how to develop a start-up budget and shows what a typical budget looks like.

Of course, every company has different start-up cash needs. Service companies have the lowest, and manufacturing companies, the highest. And, it's no longer possible to start-up in business "on a shoestring." Even those that don't need expensive equipment have to pay operating expenses from the time of starting up until the company's revenues equal its expenses.

The cash needs fall into the following categories:

■ Equipment and other permanent assets such as office furnishings, vehicles, machines and buildings.

■ Deposits. Most new companies are required to pay in advance for telephone, electricity, advertising, insurance and similar charges. All companies must pay their rent in advance.

■ Office supplies and merchandise inventory.

■ Franchise fees and similar charges. This includes the cost of forming a corporation, getting permission to do business and similar advance costs. Unlike deposits, these costs are not refunded.

■ Operating expenses for a start-up period. Business advisers recommend that new companies set aside enough money to pay operating expenses for *at least* six months, twelve months for companies that need more time to reach profitability.

■ Personal living expenses for the start-up period. Because the company may not make a profit right away, it may not be able to pay the owner a salary. So, the owner must set aside money for living expenses. This reserve should cover a longer period than the start-up to allow the owner to cover expenses if the company should fail.

■ "Cushion," an emergency reserve, discussed in the next section.

This discussion may frighten some readers about the amount of money needed to start up a company. Some readers may even decide not to go into business. Most business advisors would prefer to see entrepreneurs wait until they've accumulated enough money than to start up with inadequate funding. The budget in Figure 6-1, on Page 6-4, is an example of a start-up budget.

figure 6-1

Example - Business start-up budget

Start-up expense item	Amount
Equipment:	
Office furniture	$1,500
Fax machine	600
Telephone and installation	250
Deposits:	
Telephone	200
Electric	200
Rent	1,200
Insurance	800
Office supplies:	
Stationery with letterhead	500
Other supplies	300
Legal and accounting expenses to form corporation	1,500
Operating expenses for six months:	
Advertising	2,000
Auto and Truck	500
Insurance	800
Part-time secretary	4,000
Payroll taxes for secretary	600
Postage	600
Rent	3,600
Supplies	400
Taxes	250
Utilities and telephone	1,200
Personal living expenses for six months	10,000
(Details omitted to save space)	
Subtotal	$31,000
Reserve fund 10% of above	3,100
Total needed	$34,100

ANTICIPATING NEEDS FOR MORE MONEY

Once the company is in operation, despite thorough planning, many unexpected cash demands can happen. If the company fails to recognize, or plan for, these cash demands, it will have severe cash flow problems and may not even survive.

Thus, most start-up companies need to set aside extra money for unexpected needs. One reason a company may need this "cushion" of extra money is to finance start-up losses for longer than originally planned. Some other conditions to consider are listed below:

1. Expanding sales requires larger inventories to meet customer requirements.

2. Expanding sales results in more outstanding accounts receivable, even if collections are timely.

3. Sales growth requires additional investments in equipment and physical space.

4. Changes by competitors require changes in product line, product obsolescence, sales facilities, advertising or credit terms.

5. Seasonal fluctuations in business revenues may require additional money to purchase or build inventory in advance of seasonal rushes or to carry the company through the slow season.

6. Loan repayment schedules may strain cash balances in slow operating periods.

7. Economic conditions on a national or local basis may cause a decrease in sales or a slowing of collections from customers.

8. Inventories and accounts receivable can expand faster than sales.

9. Unexpected equipment repairs or technological changes require investment in new equipment.

The amount of this cushion depends on the type of business, size of the company, amount of risk, owner's experience, competitive market and many other factors.

CPAs recommend a cushion of at least ten percent, and up to twenty percent, of the start-up cash budget.

DEBT VERSUS EQUITY FINANCING

A company can be financed either with equity or debt. Each source has different characteristics, purposes, control and risk factors. Each source has its place in financing a business start-up.

Equity

Equity is a permanent investment of cash or property. The money can come from the company owners' funds, outside investors or reinvested business profits. Equity capital never has to be repaid. Owners and other equity investors get their money back when they sell their investments in the company.

Debt

This is money loaned to the company, or its owner, for use in the company. It has to be repaid, usually in regular installments and with interest.

DEBT FINANCING

Debt financing can be any combination of secured or unsecured financing and long-term or short-term financing.

Secured Loans v. Unsecured Loans

A secured loan is one for which the company has set aside assets to guarantee payment. The personal guarantee of the business owner is a common form of security. The owner guarantees payment on the loan in case the company cannot meet the payment schedule.

Unsecured loans to small businesses are scarce. Lenders know a small business can fail quickly and want to be assured they get paid back.

Short-Term v. Long-Term Loans

Short-term loans have to be repaid in less than one year. Long-term debts are those loans whose repayment period stretches beyond one year. Each has it own uses.

Long-term loans should be used to finance tangible assets, such as equipment, vehicles, buildings, land and even the purchase of a company. The reason long-term debt is used for these purchases is that their high cost makes it unlikely the company could repay the loans in less than one year.

Short-term loans are used to finance working capital such as accounts receivable and inventory. It is risky to use short-term borrowing to meet needs normally financed on a long-term basis. Using short-term funds for this purpose usually leads to business failure, because the company cannot meet the high payment demands.

Types of short-term debt

There are four types of short-term debt for businesses. They all are designed to meet the working capital needs of a company. Each one works a little differently. Practically every short-term loan to a small business is secured with a blanket lien, called a UCC-1, on the borrower's assets. This lien is recorded with the Secretary of State, and is part of the borrower's credit record until the loan is paid.

Short-Term Notes

These loans are issued for periods of 30, 60 and 90 days. The note is always repaid in full, with interest on the due date. Interest on short-term notes is usually discounted or subtracted from the loan proceeds at the time the money is borrowed. The effect of this standard practice is to increase the effective interest rate on the loan, as discussed later in this chapter.

Lines of Credit

After a company has shown an ability to service its debts, the bank may agree to establish a line of credit. This is a pre-approved loan for a maximum dollar amount to be used when and as needed. The interest rate varies with the bank's base interest loan rate, called the *prime rate*. The prime rate is the interest rate a bank charges its best customers: those that have good profits, solid credit ratings and excellent payment behavior.

When the company needs to draw down on the line of credit, the bank's loan officer advances any amount up to the maximum credit limit. Usually, this money is borrowed in thirty day increments and is supported by short-term notes. When a short-term note reaches maturity, it is either repaid in full or it may be renewed, or "rolled over." Most lenders require lines of credit to be repaid in full at least once per year.

Revolving Credit Agreements

Revolving credit agreements are like lines of credit. The differences are:

■ Interest is paid separately, not discounted.

■ Draw-downs are not supported by individual notes, but rather by one blanket borrowing agreement.

■ Money can be borrowed and repaid daily, a difficult procedure under a line of credit.

■ There may be no requirement for the loan to be repaid in full once per year.

Letters of Credit

These should not be confused with lines of credit. A letter of credit is not a loan. It is a guarantee made by a lender to a third party to pay a specific sum of money under specific circumstances.

A common example is the purchase of inventory. A supplier may not be willing to ship merchandise without a guarantee of payment. The customer may not be willing to pay for the goods until they are shipped. In this case, the customer asks its bank to issue a letter of credit guaranteeing payment to the supplier for the amount of the purchase.

After shipping the inventory, the supplier takes the letter of credit, invoice and shipping documents to its bank. The supplier's bank draws against the letter of credit at the customer's bank. Then, the customer's bank either charges the customer's account or makes a loan for the amount of the sale. The bank that issues the letter of credit charges its customer a commitment fee, typically 1% or 2% of the loan amount. The supplier's bank charges the supplier a fee for processing the transaction.

Sometimes, a letter of credit is not intended to be drawn upon, but just used as a payment guarantee. This is called a Standby Letter of Credit.

Types of long-term debt

There are two main types of long-term financing, term loans and mortgages. The differences include the length of the loan and the type of collateral used to secure the loan.

Term Loans

These are loans with maturity dates exceeding one year and not usually exceeding 10 years. They are paid in fixed periodic amounts, including interest. The payments can be monthly, quarterly, semi-annual or annual. Most lenders charge interest rates that float with the prime rate (described under Line of Credit). A rare few use a fixed rate.

Term loans are secured by the general credit of the company and the lender usually files a UCC-1 form to cover its position. Small businesses owners normally are required to guarantee the company's term loans. The loan agreement gives the lender a priority interest in all the assets of the company, excluding assets that have been pledged as collateral for other loans.

Installment loans are term loans that have fixed interest rates and are collateralized by specific pieces of equipment such as vehicles or machinery.

Mortgages

These are loans taken out to buy real estate. A mortgage is the only way most small businesses can borrow money for more than ten years. Commercial mortgages, unlike residential ones, usually have variable interest rates. The interest rate fluctuates with the market. The payment terms for commercial loans are also less favorable. They seldom extend over 20 years, compared to 30 years for residential loans. To make these shorter payment terms more affordable, lenders write them with longer-term payment schedules but require the loan to be paid in full in less time. Such a loan, called a "balloon" loan, might have a 30 year repayment schedule, with a final or "balloon" payment after 10 years. The lender assumes the borrower will refinance the loan or sell the property before the 10 years ends.

EQUITY FINANCING

The types of equity financing depend on the company's type of business organization. The five types of organization are discussed in Chapter 5:

- Proprietorship.
- Partnership.
- Limited Liability Company.
- "S" Corporation.
- "C" Corporation.

If a company needs outside investors to get started, the corporation or limited liability company may be the best forms, because they both shield investors from lawsuits and bankruptcies.

SOURCES OF BUSINESS CAPITAL

There are twelve main sources of capital for business start-up or expansion. Some sources work best for equity financing, and others are best for debt financing as shown in the table on the next page.

Sources of Business Capital		
Source	**Equity**	**Debt**
Personal Funds	Yes	Yes
Friends and relatives	Yes	Yes
Banks	No	Yes
Leasing	No	Yes
Suppliers	No	Yes
Asset based lenders	No	Yes
Angels	Yes	Yes
Joint ventures	Yes	Yes
Customers	No	Yes
Venture capital investors	Yes	Yes
Government backed loans	No	Yes
Government ventures	Yes	No

Personal Funds

The most common source of capital for new small businesses is the owners' savings. This source has three advantages: the interest cost is low; the money is fast and easy to get; and the money doesn't have to be repaid.

It would be a mistake for a company owner to drain the savings account for start-up money. There should be a cash reserve after business expenses are taken out. This includes cash for living expenses, children's education, personal emergencies, business problems and company expansion. Without these reserves, a company owner may have to tap the company for money; this may increase the risk of business failure. Personal financial planners recommend a reserve of six months' living expenses.

One way to conserve personal savings is to start the company as a part-time occupation, while the owner or spouse continues to work at another full-time job.

In this case, earnings from the owner's other job can cover part of the company's operating expenses.

Another source of start-up capital is the owner's retirement fund. Often, the amount of money in a pension or retirement plan is significant. This is an excellent source of capital, but there are two risks in committing all or some of it to a start-up business. One is that a company owner who is near retirement should be careful about risking a main source of retirement income on a start-up. The other is that money taken out of pension funds is heavily taxed. Besides the tax on the withdrawal, there is a 10% penalty on *premature* withdrawals from pension plans. The owner should set aside money to cover income taxes to prevent severe financial problems at tax time.

Friends and Relatives

Friends and relatives can be a source of either equity or debt financing. The possible advantages of obtaining start-up capital from them include flexible repayment terms, lower interest rates and less outside control over the company. Friends and relatives are less likely to demand control over management methods, cash levels, inventory levels, payable levels or customer credit terms.

The disadvantages of borrowing from friends and relatives center on potential personal problems if the money is not repaid on time, or if the lender encounters emergency financial needs and wants to be repaid ahead of schedule.

Most friends and relatives lend or invest based on a personal relationship and not on the soundness of a business plan. Often, they do not understand the risks they are taking. Before accepting money from friends and relatives, company owners should ask them if they are willing and financially able to lose their entire investment. If they are not, the owner should think twice before accepting the money. Many personal relationships have been ruined over business loans and investments.

The terms of loans should always be in writing, even those from friends and relatives. The Business Plan is the tool for developing the conditions surrounding personal loans, and for making sure such loans are based on economics rather than emotions.

Banks

Banks are seldom the direct source of either equity or debt for business start-ups, because they are reluctant to make loans to small businesses. However, they are an important indirect source. Many banks make personal loans or home equity loans to the owners of start-up ventures. Existing companies with profitable track records find banks a good source of financing. Some government fund sources (the Small Business Administration, for example) use banks to administer their programs. Thus, banks become the primary starting point in the search for money.

A little basic research not only saves time, but also increases the likelihood the company's loan will be approved. A partial list of factors appears below.

Type of Bank

A bank's charter limits the amount and kinds of money it can loan. Although savings banks are allowed to make business loans, commercial banks generally have more money available for businesses than savings banks.

Risk Considerations and Personal Guarantees

Regulations require banking institutions to protect against loan losses. As part of their protection policies, banks require business plans for two reasons: information about the borrower and proof that the borrower did a reasonable investigation. In addition, they request personal financial statements from the company's owners. If the borrower is a corporation, banks and other lending sources normally require the owners to guarantee the corporation's loan.

Risk Analysis

Banks conduct their own investigation of the borrower's credit worthiness, evaluate the owner's business experience, study the business plan, compare the plan's financial projections to the performance records of similar companies and evaluate the personal characteristics of the potential borrower to determine the borrower's suitability. From these reviews, banks measure the risks present in the loan request.

Approval Times

Depending upon the company's economic environment, the time required for an answer to the loan request can range from two to four weeks. Closing the transaction could add one to two weeks. If the borrower demands a quicker answer, the answer is usually "no."

Account Relationships

It is helpful to request loans from a bank where the borrower is known as a customer (depositor, checking account, mortgage holder, etc.). If the company is to be located out of the bank's market area, the loan request should be directed to a bank in its proposed location. The owner should get an introduction before sending a loan request to a bank. A CPA, attorney or a business associate who is already a customer of the bank can make the introduction.

Investigating the Bank

It is wise to investigate a bank before making a loan request, and to raise a few questions. Has the bank made loans to companies in the same business? Does the bank offer the services and have the resources to serve the business borrower? Does the bank cater to small or large companies? Is the bank in good financial condition? Who will the company be dealing with? What are the lending officer's loan approval limits? Who must approve the loan in question? Make the loan presentation to that person.

Leasing

Leasing is a popular and convenient way for small companies to obtain many types of physical assets, such as office equipment, vehicles and heavy machinery. Many manufacturers of industrial equipment offer lease purchase options as a way to increase sales. A traditional leasing arrangement requires the purchaser to make a down payment of the first and last months lease payment. Thus, the initial cash requirement is much less than if the purchaser uses a commercial bank to finance the purchase and is required to make a large down-payment.

Many leases of business property are really installment purchases. The lessor charges a rental which covers the purchase price and interest on a loan to the purchaser/lessee. When the manufacturer is the lessor, it may charge higher lease rates than third party lessors or banks. This is because the manufacturer has to guarantee the purchaser's lease payment to its own lenders and writes leases to companies with lower credit quality. Third party lessors usually specialize in specific types of equipment, require more financial information from the purchaser prior to approving the lease, have more stringent lending requirements and offer lower interest rates than manufacturers/lessors.

Suppliers

Suppliers are a good source of short term capital for small companies. There are many suppliers who are eager to help a customer grow by helping with financing. Suppliers don't usually advance money to a company; they sell products and allow extended payments of their bills. They also use their own money to develop custom applications for products. This financial help works best when there is a strong and trustworthy relationship between the supplier and its customer.

The benefit of using suppliers for start-up capital is that they usually don't charge interest on their money. The disadvantage is that the start-up company becomes a captive customer and may not be able to negotiate for the best purchase prices.

Asset Based Lenders

Asset based lenders are financial institutions that advance money against the value of liquid assets such as inventory or accounts receivable. These lenders limit their exposure by lending only a percentage (usually less than 75%) of the assets and covering only the easily liquidated assets.

Asset based lenders charge higher interest rates and require more detailed and more frequent financial reporting than traditional lenders. This is because they are accustomed to lending to weaker companies.

The asset based lending business is very competitive and diverse. Some banks offer asset based lending to their customers through separate subsidiaries. Other financial institutions specialize in one type of lending. One common specialization is accounts receivable financing, which is also known as factoring. Factoring involves the purchase of the borrower's accounts receivable; the lender collects the accounts and charges interest on the uncollected amount.

Angels

Angels are wealthy private investors who invest in small companies. Their goal is to earn higher profits on their investments than they can earn from conventional investments. Angels have the same methods and goals as venture capitalists. But, because they are investing their own money, they can act faster once they have decided to invest in a company. Angels can be found in most communities and can be located through CPAs, lawyers, venture capital clubs and local business people.

Joint Ventures with Established Companies

Lacking money to start on its own, a small company can arrange a joint venture with an established larger company. Joint ventures are common in high tech or service industries where the small company has a product or service that compliments the larger company's product line. These ventures range from research and development projects to marketing agreements for the small company's products through the larger company's marketing channels.

The benefit to the small company is faster start-up and more efficient market penetration. Another is low cost of capital compared to borrowing from a bank. The disadvantage to the smaller company is becoming too dependent on a single source of revenue or handing too much control to the larger company.

Customers

Customers are willing to finance start-up companies in three situations:

- To secure a second source of supply.
- To get access to a new or improved product.
- To get a more reliable source of supply.

Customer financing can come in the form of an outright investment, loan, joint venture or an advance payment on purchases. The benefit of getting start-up capital from customers is that they usually don't charge interest on their money. The disadvantage is that the customer may seek to control the small company's marketing efforts.

Venture Capital

Venture capitalists help companies by investing in them. They invest in start-ups, developing companies and turn-around situations. They rarely make outright loans to companies. The term *venture capital* refers to the high risk the investor takes, including the risk of a total loss. Because they take high risks, venture capitalists expect high profits on their investments. The venture capitalists' objective is to make a long-term capital gain. They usually do not expect to receive income from dividends or interest on their investments to the company, because that would drain profits from the company.

Venture capitalists can be individuals, groups of individuals or managers of funds. Fund managers invest money for individuals, pension plans, insurance companies and others. Some venture capital funds are arms of a large corporation seeking to develop or acquire new products or technologies.

In a typical start-up, there are two parties: the venture capitalist and the founding investor or inventor. The venture capitalist invests money and the founder puts up the idea or invention and the work that has gone into the company. The founder's investment is called "sweat" equity, referring to the work to get the idea started. Venture capital firms sometimes require the founder to make a capital investment in the company. The purpose of this investment is to bind the founder to the company during the difficult formative years; it would be unfortunate if the founder of a company bailed out during a start-up.

Venture capitalists monitor their investments closely. They do this through representation on the Board of Directors and by receiving regular financial reports. They may also insist on a voice in daily operations. Because of the cost of monitoring investments, venture capitalists cannot make small investments. A typical minimum limit is $500,000 to $1,000,000.

To attract a venture capitalist to invest requires sophisticated business plans and patience. In a recent survey, venture capital funds took an average of 16 weeks to make investment commitments because of their thorough review procedures. During these reviews, known as *due diligence*, the venture capital investors review everything about the company, including organization, market, products, personnel, founder's background and competition. This review process is so thorough that only a small percentage of companies actually receive funding. Before investing money, venture capitalists negotiate written agreements concerning the initial investment and future additional investments. One condition of most agreements is the right of the venture capitalists to replace the management if the company's performance is unsatisfactory.

Venture capitalists often use limited partnerships as a vehicle for handling taxes and equity problems. The partnership gives the investors, with certain limitations, tax write-offs during the start-up period and allow the outside investor to maintain control. Eventually, if the company is profitable, all partners share in the earnings. For new product or high-tech start-ups, investors can use the unique "Research and Development Limited Partnership" which provides equity capital to purchase technology. If the investment produces a successful product, the technology is sold back at a profit.

Venture capitalists receive their return on investment by selling the company back to the founder, selling to a larger company or by selling shares in the stock market. Therefore, before becoming involved with venture capitalists the company owner should be willing to give up ownership control and be willing to have others dictate the point at which the company is sold.

Venture capitalists can be located through bankers, CPAs and attorneys. They also can be found through the two chapters, Hartford and Stamford, of the Connecticut Venture Capital Network. In addition to firms located in Connecticut, venture capital firms located in other states often are willing to make investments in Connecticut.

Government Backed Loans

The State and Federal governments both have many loan programs for small companies. Between them, they have formed many federal, state, and local agencies to help small companies, particularly during recent difficult times. At the federal level, the Small Business Administration (SBA) and the Small Business Development Center (SBDC) provide loan programs and management help, respectively. At the state level, most of the aid is coordinated through the Connecticut Department of Economic Development. A more detailed list and discussion of specific programs follows later in this chapter.

Government Ventures

There are fewer government equity programs than there are loan programs. The SBA runs one, the Small Business Investment Company (SBIC) Program, discussed later in this chapter. Connecticut runs several programs through the Department of Economic Development, discussed later in the chapter.

HOW LENDERS CHARGE FOR LOANS

Banks and other lenders earn money from the interest and fees they charge borrowers. They use the prime lending rate as a starting point. A safe loan is made at the prime rate. A more risky loan is made at a premium over the prime rate. A risky borrower also pays higher fee charges. A good place to start is with terminology:

■   There are two ways that interest can be charged: at *floating rates* or at *fixed rates*.

■   There are also two ways to figure interest charges on a loan: *simple interest* and *discounted interest*. The method used has a significant effect on the cost of a loan.

Floating rate loans

These loans have their rates tied to a base rate such as the bank's prime rate, the prime rate published in the *Wall Street Journal* or the United States Treasury Note rate. Interest rates are expressed in relation to the base rate. Thus, a rate of "prime plus 2" means the bank adds 2 percentage points to the prime rate. If the prime rate is 8%, the customer pays 10%. The rate is subject to frequent changes.

Fixed rate loans

These loans have interest rates that do not change over the life of the loan. To cover their risk, lenders boost the rate for fixed rate loans slightly over the current floating rate.

Simple Interest

This is a method of calculating interest by multiplying the yearly interest rate by current loan balance. Adjustments are made to the actual dollar amount of interest based upon the number of days the current loan balance is outstanding, using a 360 day year.

Discounted interest

When interest is discounted, it is subtracted from the loan proceeds at the time the money is borrowed. *This standard practice increases the effective interest rate on the loan, because the loan proceeds are less than the amount borrowed.* The lending industry uses a standard practice of calculating loan interest based upon a 360 day year, which further increases the effective interest rate.

The example below illustrates how the amount of interest and the effective interest rate are calculated under the two different methods.

Comparison of simple and discounted interest		
	Simple	Discounted
Interest rate	10.0%	10.0%
Term of loan	1 year	1 year
Amount borrowed	10,000	10,000
Interest deducted	0	1,000
Net amount received	10,000	9,000
Amount paid as interest	1,000	1,000
Rate of interest on money borrowed	10.0%	11.1%

Fees and Points

Fees and points are charged by lenders as a means of increasing the income on a loan without raising the stated interest rate.

Points are an advance fee designed to pay for the lender's cost of processing the loan paperwork. Points are expressed as a percentage of the loan amount, so a fee of two points on a $100,000 loan would cost the borrower $2,000.

A *commitment fee* is a charge to establish a lending arrangement that is available for future use. Commitment fees are common for letters of credit and revolving credit lines. When the borrower actually draws on a revolving credit line or letter of credit, it pays a usage fee in addition to the usual interest charge. This usage fee is typically less than 1% of the amount of the loan.

The actual interest rate, amount and types of fees charged by a lender varies, depending on the borrower's credit worthiness. They also depend on the amount of money a bank has available to lend, which is influenced by government regulations and the bank's financial condition.

PREPARING A PROPOSAL FOR FINANCING

Most lenders and investors require detailed information packages before they can consider advancing money. This package allows them to evaluate their chance of getting their money back and making a profit. More important, the package allows them to decide between competing uses for their money. A company that seeks funding must develop a proposal which persuades an investor or lender to advance money to it, rather than to other companies.

The typical complete financing package should contain the following information:

- **Business Plan** - the business plan describes the company in detail, including the history, future plans, products or services, its industry, competitors, business strategy and key management. For a detailed discussion and example of a business plan, see Chapter 4, *Business Planning*.

- **Loan Request** - The loan request describes the amount of money being requested, the proposed terms, use of proceeds, sources of repayment, available collateral and a repayment schedule.

- **Cash flow Projections** - The cash flow projection shows future sources of cash from the company's normal operations, cash requirements to meet operating expenses and capital purchases, uses of money and projected payback schedule.

- **Financial Statements** - For an existing company, financial statements for the past three years of the company, including balance sheet, statements of income and retained earnings, and a statement of cash flows. The owners' personal financial statements or copies of their income tax returns should be included, too.

- **Other Information** - any other information which may be of use in evaluating the loan request, such as owners' résumés, press releases, promotional materials, and product samples should be included.

The financing proposal should explain any unfavorable aspects of the company's past. These include bankruptcies, liens, loan defaults, slow payment history and lawsuits. If these are discovered during a credit check or financial review, they could kill the company's chances, if they were not previously disclosed. By dealing with negative items early in the process, the company can present the favorable side of the story.

GETTING OUTSIDE HELP WITH THE FINANCING PROCESS

Depending upon the size of the company, its prior loan experience and its financial sophistication, management may want to obtain outside experience in dealing with credit grantors or investors. Most financial institutions view the use of outside help favorably and not as a sign of weakness. Third parties can help in preparing the loan package, negotiating terms, and providing introductions to money sources. Among those qualified to help the company owner are CPAs, attorneys, the Service Core of Retired Executives, Community Accounting Aid and Services, Inc. and the Connecticut Small Business Development Center.

SMALL BUSINESS ADMINISTRATION PROGRAMS

The principal source of the Federal Government support for small business is the U.S. Small Business Administration founded in 1953. The SBA's objective is to generate and preserve jobs.

The Department of Commerce and the Department of Agriculture have programs similar to those of the SBA. New or early-stage companies should work through the SBA, which can then direct them to other agencies if necessary. Starting with the SBA shortens the overall time in getting a helping hand.

SBA Loan proceeds may be used to establish a new company or to help in the operation, acquisition, or expansion of an existing company, including working capital; the purchase of inventory; machinery and equipment; and the construction, expansion and rehabilitation of business property.

Loan proceeds may not be used for: partial purchase of a company; funding lending institutions; real estate held for investment, speculation or rental; opinion molders such as magazines, newspapers, trade journals, radio or television; live entertainment; schools; religious organizations and their affiliates.

To be eligible for SBA loan help, a company must qualify under SBA size criteria. For business loans, eligibility depends on the average number of employees or on sales volume.

The standards vary with the type of business:

■   **Manufacturing**   Maximum number of employees may range from 500 to 1500, depending on the type of product manufactured.

■   **Wholesaling**   Maximum number of employees may not exceed 100.

■   **Services**   Annual receipts may not exceed $3.5 to $14.5 million, depending on the industry.

■   **Retailing**   Annual receipts may not exceed $3.5 to $14.5 million, depending on the industry.

■   **Construction**   General construction annual receipts may not exceed $9.5 to $17 million, depending on the industry.

■   **Special Trade Construction**   Annual Receipts may not exceed $7 million.

■   **Agriculture**   Annual receipts may not exceed $0.5 to $3.5 million, depending on the industry.

Following its mandate, the SBA's financial support to the nation's small businesses is offered through three programs:

1. 7(a) loan program.
2. Certified Development Company Program.
3. Small Business Investment Company (SBIC) Program.

The details of these programs can be found later in this chapter.

Currently, most SBA loans are in the form of guarantees to loans made by private lenders, usually banks, and guaranteed to a maximum of 90% by the SBA. The maximum guarantee on loans exceeding $155,000 is 85%. The SBA can guarantee up to $750,000 of a private sector loan. The SBA does not make direct "grants" of money for starting a small business.

The SBA has a limited amount of money available for direct loans (up to a maximum of $150,000) which are available only to applicants unable to secure an SBA guaranteed loan. This money is available only to certain types of borrowers (i.e.; businesses located in high-unemployment areas, or owned by low-income individuals, handicapped individuals, Vietnam veterans or disabled persons).

The SBA requires a business plan to be part of any loan request package. It requires sufficient assets be pledged to adequately secure the loan to the extent they are available. Personal guarantees are required of all principal owners and from the chief executive officer of the company, regardless of ownership interest. Liens on personal assets of the principals also may be required, where business assets are considered insufficient to secure the loan.

In order to take advantage of the SBA guaranteed loan programs, the company needs time. A typical time schedule takes 15 weeks from starting until the money is available:

- Preparation time for business plan: 2 to 4 weeks.
- Bank's determination: 2 to 3 weeks.
- SBA Guarantee process: 1 to 2 weeks.
- Direct SBA loan, additional time: 2 to 3 weeks.

SBA 7(a) loan program

The 7(a) loan program is the largest of the SBA's financial assistance programs, making up over 80% of all SBA business lending activity. This program includes three types of loans: guarantee, direct and immediate participation.

Guarantee Loans

Guarantee loans are made and disbursed by private lenders and guaranteed by the SBA. If a borrower defaults on a guaranteed loan, the SBA purchases an agreed-upon percentage of the unpaid balance of the loan. By law, the SBA can guarantee a maximum of $750,000. There is no minimum amount; however, most commercial lenders are reluctant to process loans of less than $25,000. The guarantee percentage depends on the type of loan discussed in the next two sections.

Loans not exceeding $155,000

The SBA must guarantee 90% of all loans under $155,000 except where loan proceeds are used to refinance existing debt, in which case the SBA guarantees a maximum of 80%. If only part of the loan is for debt payment, the guarantee percentage is determined on a pro rated basis, whereby the debt payment portion of the loan is guaranteed anywhere between a maximum of 80% to a minimum of zero, as illustrated on the following page.

EXAMPLE

The company seeks a $100,000 loan of which $30,000 is for refinancing the company and $70,000 is for new programs.

Maximum	$70,000 "new money"	X	90% =	$63,000
Guarantee	$30,000 refinancing	X	80% =	24,000
				$87,000

Minimum	$70,000 "new money"	X	90% =	$63,000
Guarantee	$30,000 refinancing	X	0% =	None

Maximum percent: $87,000 ÷ $100,000 =   87%

Minimum percent: $63,000 ÷ $100,000 =   63%

Thus, the permissible SBA guarantee percentage on this loan ranges from 63% to 87%.

Loans exceeding $155,000

The SBA can guarantee a maximum of 85% and a minimum of 70% of loans exceeding $155,000, except when part or all of the loan proceeds are used to refinance existing debt. In this case the rules enumerated above apply with the new money having a guarantee of 85%. When a 70% participation causes the SBA's exposure to exceed $750,000, a lesser guarantee is permitted as long as the SBA's exposure is limited to $750,000.

When a Guarantee Loan is approved, the participating lender pays the SBA a guarantee fee. The fee is usually passed onto the borrower and may be paid from the loan proceeds. This fee is assessed on the guaranteed part of the loan and the fee percent depends on the loan maturity. The fee is 2% of loans over one year and ¼% of loans under one year.

Direct loans

Direct loans are available only to borrowers who are unable to obtain lender participation loans. Although the legal ceiling on direct loans is $350,000, the SBA has set an administrative ceiling for these loans of $150,000. Direct loan applications in excess of $150,000 can only be accepted with the approval of the Regional Administrator. Because of present funding limitations, direct loans are available only to certain categories of borrowers. These include Vietnam-era and disabled veterans, the handicapped, low-income borrowers and businesses located in high unemployment areas. To qualify for direct loans, borrowers must be able to prove they were turned down on a good faith financing request to a private lender (or two lenders in cities of 20,000 people or more). The SBA and the borrower negotiate the terms of direct loans, subject to the SBA's policy and lending requirements.

Immediate participation loans

Immediate Participation (IP) loans are those made jointly by SBA and private lenders whereby either the SBA or the participating lender makes the loan. Upon disbursement, the other participant immediately purchases its agreed-upon share of the loan. These loans can be serviced either by the lender or by the SBA. IP loans are permissible, subject to funding availability, only when a guarantee loan is unavailable. The SBA's participation is limited to 75% or $150,000, whichever is less, except in cases where a participant's legal limit precludes a 25% participation. Because of direct funding limitations, this program is seldom used.

SBA loan provisions

The terms of Guaranty and Immediate Participation loans are negotiated between the applicant and the participating financial institution, subject to approval by the SBA. The SBA and the borrower negotiate the terms of Direct Loans, subject to SBA policy and lending standards. The loan can be of any amount so long as the SBA-guaranteed portion of the loan (or combination of all outstanding loans to any one borrower) does not exceed $750,000. Direct Loans (or combination of all outstanding direct loans to any one borrower) cannot exceed $150,000, except when a waiver is obtained from the Regional Office, in which case this maximum is $350,000.

Loan maturity varies with the economic life of the assets being financed and the applicant's ability to repay, subject to the following maximums:

USE	MAXIMUM MATURITY
Working Capital	up to 5-7 years
Machinery and Equipment	up to 7-10 years
Building Construction or Purchase	up to 25 years

When loan proceeds are used for a combination of purposes, the maximum maturity can be a weighted average of the maturities or a sum of equal monthly installments for all the maturities. The weighted average produces a level payment for the life of the loan. The sum of the maturities produces unequal installment payments.

The interest rate for Guaranteed Loans reflects prevailing market rates. It can be a fixed or variable rate. The maximum interest rate permitted on Guaranty Loans is the prime rate published in the *Wall Street Journal* plus 2.25% for loans maturing in under seven years and up to 2.75% for loans maturing in over seven years. Direct loans are made at a fixed rate which is set quarterly by the SBA.

The SBA also charges the lender a 2% guaranty fee, based upon the amount of the guaranteed portion of the loan. SBA policy allows the lender to charge this guarantee to the borrower and it should be considered part of the loan cost.

SBA loan application procedures

The application process for an SBA loan is like that for a bank loan. The SBA deals with the private lender, not the applicant. The applicant submits a financing request to a participating bank. Not all banks participate in the SBA's loan programs. If the lender cannot make the loan directly, it submits the loan to the SBA under the guarantee program. If the lender cannot make the SBA guaranteed loan, a qualified applicant may then apply for a direct loan from the SBA.

SBA special loan programs

The SBA has three other loan programs: 7(a)11 Loan Program, Certified Development Company Program (CDC) and Small Business Investment Company Program, and described below.

7(a)11 Loan Program

Companies located in high-unemployment or low-income areas, as well as companies owned by low-income individuals, are eligible for the SBA's Direct Loan program. To qualify, a company must be located in an area designated by the Department of Labor as having severe or persistent unemployment or must be more than 50% owned by low-income individuals -- defined for the purpose of this program as those individuals having inadequate income to meet basic family needs.

Certified Development Company Program (CDC)

The CDC program is an economic development loan program to help in the development and expansion of small firms and the creation of jobs. This program is designed to provide fixed-asset financing to small businesses for the construction or rehabilitation of owner-occupied or leased premises.

Eligible small businesses are those with a net worth under $6,000,000 and average annual net profits after taxes over the past two years under $2,000,000, or which qualify under the SBA's size standards. Companies doing business in media, gambling, lending or investment, and non-profit concerns are not eligible. An applicant purchasing existing commercial real estate must occupy a minimum of 51% of the building's area, and an applicant constructing new commercial real estate must occupy at least 85% of the building's area.

Loan proceeds may be used for plant acquisition, construction, conversion, or expansion; for the rehabilitation of commercial structures; and for the purchase and installation of machinery and equipment with a useful life of ten years or more. In addition, certain "soft costs" may be paid with loan proceeds, including: interim interest costs and professional fees for items such as; appraisals, surveying, accounting, engineering, and architectural services.

The SBA's share of the loan amount cannot exceed $750,000 or 40% of the total project cost, whichever is less. Loan maturity can be 10, 15, 20 or 25 years.

This program is administered through SBA-Certified Development Companies and requires a 10% investment from either the CDC or the borrower. A private or a non-federal governmental financial institution provides an independent first loan of at least 50% of the project cost, and the SBA, through the guarantee of a CDC debenture, provides a second loan for up to 40% of the project cost or $500,000, whichever is less.

The interest rate is fixed. CDC debentures are sold through the private capital markets and reflect the prevailing market rate at the time the debenture is sold by the SBA.

Small Business Investment Company (SBIC) Program

The SBA's Small Business Investment Company (SBIC) program provides long-term loans and/or venture capital to small firms. SBICs are privately-owned investment companies, which are licensed and regulated by the SBA. Because money for venture or risk investments is difficult for small firms to obtain, the SBA provides financial help to SBICs to stimulate and supplement the flow of private equity and long-term loan money to small companies. Venture capitalists participate in the SBIC program to supplement their own private capital with money borrowed at favorable rates through the SBA's guarantee of SBIC debentures, which are sold to private investors.

The SBA also licenses Minority Enterprise SBICs (MESBICs), which specialize in meeting the needs of small firms owned by socially or economically disadvantaged persons.

An SBIC's success is linked to the growth and profitability of the companies it finances. As a result, some SBICs primarily help companies with significant growth potential, such as new firms in innovative industries. SBICs finance small firms by providing straight loans and/or equity-type investments. These equity investments often give SBICs partial ownership of those companies in the hope of sharing in the companies' profits as they grow and prosper. The following types of investments are commonly used by SBICs:

- **Loans with Warrants**: SBICs may make loans in return for warrants. Warrants enable SBICs to purchase common stock, usually at a favorable price, during a specific period of time.

- **Convertible Debentures**: SBICs may make loans with a conversion feature whereby the debenture can be converted (or exchanged) at the SBIC's option, into an equivalent amount of common stock.

- **Stock**: SBICs may purchase common or preferred stock from the company.

Some SBICs also provide management help to the companies they finance to help foster the company's growth and as protection for the SBIC's investment.

Eligible small businesses are those with a net worth not exceeding $6 million and average annual net profits after taxes over the past two years not to exceed $2 million, or which qualify under SBA's size standards. The terms of investment are negotiated by the SBIC and the small business concern. Generally, financing is for at least 5 years.

Interest rates on SBIC loans are limited by SBA regulation and depend upon the security offered and the company's earnings and are negotiated between the SBIC and the small business, subject to the legal ceiling (if any) of the State in which the SBIC is organized.

Firms interested in raising venture capital should be referred to local SBICs, which are listed in the SBIC directory published semiannually by the SBA, and should be encouraged to investigate them, looking for such things as what types of financing they provide, what types of businesses they invest in, how much money is available, and if they offer management help. Most SBICs need a business plan, including past and current financial statements, to evaluate any proposal for financing. Inquiries about information and licensing of new SBICs and MESBICs should be referred to the SBA's Office of Investment (Central Office).

FINANCING AND MANAGEMENT ASSISTANCE PROGRAMS

Small companies are a government priority. From them comes a large part of the nation's technical innovation and new jobs. For that reason, there are thousands of state and federal programs to help small companies with money and advice. Most of these programs are open to all small companies, but a few are restricted to those owned by minority groups, women and veterans.

FEDERAL ASSISTANCE

There are many programs within the Federal Government which promote the interests of the small business. Most agencies have offices which specifically serve the interests of minority or women-owned companies. Listed below are a few of these offices. For a more comprehensive listing of Federal programs, contact the State's Office of Small Businesses Services, the CSBDC, the Chamber of Commerce, or consult the *Handbook for Small Business: A Survey of Small Business Programs of the Federal Government*, available in most libraries.

Department of Agriculture

The Department of Agriculture has established the Office of Small and Disadvantaged Business Utilization which serves small business interests as well as minority and women owned business interests. One of its major objectives is to provide a liaison for small businesses and government programs designed to make business opportunities available to them (e.g., the Procurement Preference Programs and Labor Surplus Area programs). In addition, this office publishes informational brochures for small businesses, provides outreach seminars, and coordinates Department of Agriculture programs with those of other agencies which serve the small business interest.

Department of Commerce

The Department of Commerce serves minority business interests with the Minority Business Development Agency. This agency has over 100 Minority Business Development Centers around the country which provide management, marketing and technical help for minority business owners.

Department of Education

The Department of Education offers business opportunities to small businesses performing the six following services:

1. Management consulting.
2. Program evaluations.
3. Computer-based projects.
4. Student testing materials.
5. Productions of audio-visual materials.
6. Other professional services.

General Services Administration

Most major purchases for the Federal government go through the General Services Administration. This is an excellent source of business opportunities for small businesses. The General Services Administration runs regional business service centers, which counsel companies on government contracting opportunities. Personnel from the Business Service Centers also make trips, usually sponsored through local chambers of commerce, to communities to explain programs. These counseling centers make efforts to locate and contact minority and women-owned businesses to encourage them to bid on proposals.

Department of the Interior

The Department of the Interior, Bureau of Indian Affairs, maintains several field offices which provide information on the Tribal Resources Development Program. The Bureau also provides financing information for Native-American business owners.

Department of Labor

The Women's Bureau of the Department of Labor seeks to expand business opportunities for women-owned companies, as well as serving to promote the welfare of women workers. In addition, the Department of Labor has an Office of Small and Disadvantaged Business Utilization which provides help and information to small businesses on labor topics.

Minority Business Development Agency

This agency provides help to minority entrepreneurs who need assistance in starting a company. Its services include putting minority business owners in contact with other government programs and acting as a source of catalogs, publications and other information concerning minority business. The regional office which serves Connecticut is in New York at 26 Federal Plaza, New York, NY 10278.

Small Business Administration

Besides its loan programs, the Small Business Administration manages several programs to help small business owners in running their companies. One is the Connecticut Small Business Development Center (CSBDC), discussed in this chapter under State Assistance.

The SBA's Office of Minority Small Business and Capital Ownership Development serves as an advocate for minority small businesses in terms of government policy and law making. In addition, it coordinates resources available to minority businesses, helps in obtaining cooperation among other agencies in terms of government programs available for minority businesses, monitors the performance and examines the problems specific to minority-owned businesses.

The SBA's Office of Women's Business Ownership serves women-owned businesses by seeking greater opportunities for participation in government and private business programs. The Office promotes procurement goals for women-owned businesses, sponsors national conferences for women, and collects data on women-owned businesses.

STATE ASSISTANCE

The primary source of state assistance for small, women-owned and minority-owned companies comes from the Connecticut State Department of Economic Development. This department administers several programs and offices:

- Business Outreach Centers.

- Office of Small Business Services.

- Connecticut Development Authority.
  - Third party loans.
  - Direct loans.

- Connecticut Innovations, Inc.

- Community Economic Development Fund.

The number of available assistance funds changes regularly, so it is a good idea to check with CAAS or CSBDC for an update.

Business Outreach Centers

The Business Outreach Centers are a network of offices that provide general consulting and educational programs which meet the needs of small businesses for financing, marketing, tax requirements and managerial skills. These offices provide personalized managerial help for small businesses of all kinds, in any stage of planning, start-up or maturity. The Centers help with business plans, managerial methods, sales and market planning, business strategies and operating functions such as marketing, personnel and accounting.

The Business Outreach Centers also serve as the liaison between the entrepreneur and the programs sponsored by the Department of Economic Development. They serve this function by helping in the preparation of business plans required by State and Federal loan request programs.

Office of Small Business Services

The Department's Office of Small Business Services oversees the *Set-Aside Program*, which gives 25% of state government purchases and contracts to Connecticut small businesses. Of the total amount reserved for small businesses, 25% is set aside for minority and women-owned businesses.

The Office of Small Business Services also publishes a directory of Connecticut women in business and a directory of minority-owned businesses. These directories are available to government offices and businesses so they can buy from the state's women and minority-owned businesses.

Connecticut Development Authority Third Party loans

A third party loan is one the borrower or the CDA arrange with a conventional lender and that is guaranteed by the CDA. One benefit of this type of loan is that it can often be arranged more quickly than can a direct CDA loan. The CDA has five third party programs. They all require the borrower to pay a one-time application and commitment fee and to pay an annual guarantee fee from ½% to 2½%, depending on the extent of the guarantee.

Connecticut Works Guarantee Program

This is a broad lending program for loans up to $25,000,000. Under this program, the CDA finances revolving lines of credit, term loans and fixed asset loans. The CDA also finances owner-occupied commercial real estate construction and handles refinancing in most cases.

Connecticut Small Business Reserve/URBANK

This fund provides loan loss reserves to banks to encourage them to make small loans to businesses that create or retain jobs in seven economic areas: Bridgeport, Hartford, New Haven, Stamford, Waterbury, New London County and Windham County.

CT Business Development Corp

This is the certified statewide development company that sponsors the federal Small Business Administration 504 Program to offer low-cost, long-term fixed-rate loans for established small businesses. The company finances up to 40% of project cost up to $1,000,000 for the purchase of buildings and equipment. To be eligible, the company must be an established business, have sales less than $6,000,000 and net income less than $2,000,000.

Self-Sustaining Bonds

Through this program, the CDA arranges to sell taxable and tax-exempt bonds, up to $10,000,000, for major economic development projects, including manufacturing facilities, water facilities, solid waste disposal and similar projects.

Mortgage and Loan Insurance Fund

This fund guarantees up to 100% of bank loans for economic development projects for manufacturing and other businesses contributing significantly to Connecticut's economic base. It covers: real estate up to $25,000,000; equipment up to $10,000,000; and working capital up to $10,000,000.

Connecticut Development Authority Direct loans

A direct loan is one the CDA makes directly to the borrower. A direct loan is intended to be the borrower's last resort; in order to get one, the borrower must first be refused by conventional lenders. The CDA has seven direct loan funds.

Connecticut Works Fund

This fund is the direct counterpart of the Connecticut Works Guarantee Program. Through this fund, companies can receive direct loans and custom guarantees for economic development projects. Eligible borrowers include companies that are unable to obtain conventional financing, unable to participate in other CDA programs, or significantly enhance Connecticut's economic base. The fund provides up to $25,000,000 in loans and up to $15,000,000 in loan guarantees.

Growth Fund

This fund provides direct state loans to small business for buildings and working capital up to $4,000,000. To be eligible, the borrower must have annual sales less than $25,000,000, and not be able to get conventional bank financing.

Investment Finance

This fund offers direct loans and investments to growing businesses with strong potential for high job and economic growth for Connecticut. The fund provides up to $1,000,000 in investments and loans to companies that are high-tech, high value added, have strong export sales, strong job growth or are in second stage market development.

Special Purpose Financing

This fund provides direct state loans up to $250,000 for buildings, equipment and working capital for specialized projects such as:

■   Small water companies and dams. publicly or privately owned.

■   Contractors and enterprise zone businesses with sales under $3,000,000.

■   Loans up to $1,000,000 to businesses impacted by natural disasters or economic emergency.

Naugatuck Valley Fund

The CDA administers loans from a special federal fund for buildings, equipment and working capital for manufacturing or distribution companies located in the Naugatuck Valley and certain other towns. The maximum loan is $250,000, and matching bank or equity funding is required on a 2:1 basis.

Environmental Clean-up Fund

This provides loans up to $200,000 to business property owners unable to obtain clean-up financing from conventional sources, and for the development of clean alternatively powered vehicles. Eligible business must have been established at least one year in Connecticut, have sales less than $3,000,000 or employment less than 150.

Environmental Assistance Fund

This provides loans, or loan guarantees, up to $250,000 for projects approved by the Hazardous Waste Management Service that reduce the use of hazardous and toxic substances through production process changes. To be eligible, a company must have 150 employees or less, or gross revenues of less than $25,000,000

Connecticut Innovations, Inc.

Connecticut Innovations, Inc. (CII) provides financing for new product development and encourages businesses, start-up ventures and entrepreneurs to turn innovative ideas into new products and processes. CII financing provides up to 60% of the eligible development costs of specific projects from initial concept through fabrication of the production-ready prototype. Importantly, CII does not request a share in company ownership or management. Instead, CII requires only a limited royalty on the sales of the products it finances. In addition, to help get new products produced, marketed and sold, CII also offers low-cost loans of up to $200,000.

Community Economic Development Fund

The Community Economic Development Fund, created in September of 1993, is the nation's first state-sponsored lending institution created to finance business start-ups and other development in poor areas. The fund is designed to provide financing to businesses denied through traditional bank channels. Organized as two separate business entities, it writes loans and provides financial services such as mortgage insurance and loan programs through a for-profit corporation and assists in the writing of business plans and marketing products through its not-for-profit counterpart.

Other state assistance

Throughout Connecticut, growth-oriented business owners can find help from their local chambers of commerce, town economic development agencies, utility companies and regional development agencies. In competition to gain and retain jobs, these groups have developed innovative programs to help their business partners. At the state level, there are two groups that have a state-wide reach: Community Accounting Aid and Services, Inc. and The Connecticut Small Business Development Center

Connecticut Small Business Development Center

CSBDC is a statewide organization with a full-time staff of professional consultants who provide confidential, one-on-one business consulting services to small business owners throughout the state. Headquartered at the University of Connecticut, the CSBDC has offices in West Hartford, Groton, Norwich, Willimantic, Danielson, New Haven, Stamford, Bridgeport and Waterbury, and also provides counseling in Danbury, Enfield, Torrington, Middletown, and Hartford through local Chambers of Commerce. All consulting services are provided without cost, but an appointment is necessary. Assistance is available in such areas as business planning, marketing strategies, record keeping, financial analysis and loan packaging. Funding for the services provided through the CSBDC comes from a mix of sources including the U.S. Small Business Administration, the University of Connecticut and the private sector. The CSBDC also sponsors numerous small business workshops each year, and operates a number of specialized service centers including an Export Center, Business Research Law Clinic and Manufacturing Technology Assistance Center.

Community Accounting Aid and Services, Inc.

CAAS is a related state-wide organization that is sponsored by the accounting profession and CSBDC. Working through a small permanent staff, CAAS arranges for professional accountants to volunteer their time to help eligible business owners. Assistance includes developing business plans, training, start-up support and similar assignments.

Other sources of assistance

In addition to the local, state and federal help described above, there are national business organizations for both minorities and women. There is the American Association of Minority Enterprise Small Business Investment Companies (Washington, D.C.), Americans for Indian Opportunity (Washington, D.C.), Associated Minority Contractors of America (Washington, D.C.), Interracial Council for Business Opportunity (New York), to name only a few. A few examples for women are the American Business Women's Association (Kansas City, MO), Women Entrepreneurs (San Francisco, CA), and the National Association of Women Business Owners (Washington, D.C.). Directories of associations and business organizations are helpful in locating the appropriate agencies.

OPPORTUNITIES FOR MINORITIES AND WOMEN

Minority-owned and women-owned businesses are specifically encouraged by both local and federal organizations. In addition to the help available to any small business, additional offices or agencies are set up to offer special help to minority and women-owned businesses.

There are a variety of sources for funding, managerial help, educational programs and consulting available to minority and women-owned businesses. The question is how to locate and make use of the help which is available. There are several paths one can take to discover how to use the programs which exist. Often, the easiest and first step in locating help is to check local offerings. Many local sources may prove to be the bridge in locating state and federal help.

Chambers of Commerce

Local chambers of commerce, especially those located in larger metropolitan areas, provide help and information to start-up companies, especially those owned by minority group members and women. Local chambers also form self-help networks for small business owners. Through these networks, owners meet and discuss problems and opportunities.

Hartford Economic Development Corporation

HEDCO is a nonprofit organization serving the Greater Hartford area. Its main purpose is to help minority and women-owned businesses to get financing. It also serves as a source of information for all businesses.

Libraries

Public libraries and university and college libraries offer many business publications, books, and reference materials for all small business owners.

CONCLUSION

The financing for a small company is a critical aspect of starting up. Without enough money to start, *and keep going through the start-up period*, the company can't survive. This aspect of start-up demands plenty of planning and work.

Still, there is plenty of money out there for qualified, hard working business owners. They must take the time to find the money in the many government programs and departments. And, they must understand that these programs are not handouts. They are loan programs, and the lenders expect to get their money back to lend to other small business start-ups.

Chapter 7
Business Record-keeping

INTRODUCTION

There are many factors that determine the success of a company: financing, competition, marketing and the economy. However, the main measure of success is the numbers. The company's records are the *only* source of this financial information.

Good records allow business managers to analyze their successes and plan for the future. They allow banks and investors to understand business results. Finally, good records are essential for complete and accurate business tax returns.

Poor records, on the other hand, seriously undermine business managers' credibility with banks, investors and the Internal Revenue Service. Poor records can lead to lost tax write-offs and higher tax penalties and assessments. Finally, poor records prevent managers from controlling the company.

ORGANIZATION OF CHAPTER

Components of a good record-keeping system
Practical forms of business records
Computer systems
Managing and summarizing information
Using accounting data to manage
How to improve the company's records

COMPONENTS OF A GOOD RECORD-KEEPING SYSTEM

There is no universally correct records system. The system's structure must be tailored to fit the needs of the company. There is only one universal objective: to keep the system as simple as possible. A well-designed system will pay for itself by reducing bookkeeping time and accounting fees and by providing essential information for effective business management.

There are many sources of help for records system design, including the company's CPA firm, one-write system vendors, business counsellors from Community Accounting Aid and Services, the Connecticut Small Business Development Center and computer consultants.

There are six basic business records. Most companies should use them all, although the form will vary considerably between companies. Accountants refer to these records as the *books of original entry* because they are the source of all other business documents, including tax returns and financial statements. These basic records are:

- Sales.
- Cash receipts.
- Purchases.
- Cash disbursements.
- Payroll.
- General journal.

In a larger company, these records may be subdivided into many components. For example, a manufacturer might have a different sales record for each type of product line or each type of customer. In a small company, it is possible to combine some records, such as payrolls and cash disbursements. Some, such as the sales journal, may not even be needed in a small company.

This section discusses the purpose, and shows an example of a simple version, of each type of business record. Accountants use the terms *journals* and *ledgers* to refer to these records. The term *books*, used interchangeably in this chapter, means the same thing.

Sales journal

This journal records each sale of goods or services. Its purpose is to keep track of sales, amounts due from customers and the Connecticut sales tax collected from customers. It is a record of the individual invoices or sales slips from customers. If the company sells on credit, the sales record allows it to keep track of the customer name and amount owed for each sale.

An example of a simple sales journal is shown in Figure 7-1 on Page 7-3.

figure 7-1

Example - Sales Journal

Date	Invoice	Customer	Taxable	Nontaxable	Tax	Total
9/01	101	Peerless Widget Co.	500.00		30.00	530.00
9/01	102	John S. Peters	175.50		10.53	186.03
9/01	103	City of Hartford		1000.00	.00	1000.00
9/30	316	Kyle Wayne	200.00		12.00	212.00
9/30	317	Cynthia Jones	250.00		15.03	265.53
9/30	318	David Smith	600.00		36.00	636.00
Total			50100.00	10000.00	3006.00	63106.00

One important purpose of the sales journal is to record transactions on which sales taxes must be collected. The Connecticut sales tax report form requires companies to start with their total sales and to show deductions for transactions that are not taxable. The deductions must be explained on the sales tax form. Most companies can complete the sales tax form by summarizing the *nontaxable* column of the sales journal. Companies that have many different types of exempt sales may need to have several *nontaxable* columns.

Likewise, if the company sells several types of services or products, it may need to expand the number of columns to accommodate the main types.

A related record is the *accounts receivable record*. This record keeps track of amounts due from customers. Typically, one record is kept for each customer, either on a 5" x 8" card or on 8½" x 11" paper. When a sale is made to a customer, it is posted to the customer's record, adding to the customer's balance. When a payment is received, it is deducted from the balance. The card can be copied and mailed to customers as a reminder notice.

An example of a simple accounts receivable ledger card is shown in Figure 7-2, on Page 7-4.

figure 7-2

Example - Accounts receivable ledger

Customer name	John S. Peters			
Customer Number	12345			

Date	Invoice	Sale	Receipt	Balance
9/01	Balance Forward			500.00
9/01	102	186.03		686.03
9/17	165	450.00		1136.03
9/18	166	200.00		1336.03
9/20			500.00	836.03
9/22	253	400.00		1236.03
9/25			100.00	1136.03
9/26	269	150.00		1286.03

For "cash sale" businesses like grocery stores, retail shops and restaurants, the sales journal and accounts receivable record are not necessary, because the cash receipts journal contains all the necessary information. When the cash journal is used as the main sales record, it must be modified to capture the necessary sales tax information.

Cash receipts journal

Every company has to have a cash receipts journal to record the money it receives. Like the sales journal, the cash receipts journal records every deposit of money in a useful format for tax and business analysis. The source of the receipt is important information. Cash receipts sources normally fall into three groups: (1) cash from credit customers in payment of their accounts, (2) cash from cash sales, and (3) cash from miscellaneous sources. Sales receipts must be identified separately from bank loan proceeds, transfers from other cash accounts, money invested in the company, insurance claims, vendor refunds and similar non-business receipts. Poor records could result in sales taxes or income taxes being paid on money that should not be taxable.

An example of a simple cash receipts journal and sample entries is shown in Figure 7-3, on Page 7-5.

figure 7-3

Example - Cash receipts journal

Date	Invoice	Customer	Sales	Sales Tax	Other	Total
9/01	103	City of Hartford	1000.00			1000.00
9/01		National Bank loan			5000.00	5000.00
9/01	102	John S. Peters	100.00			100.00
9/29		Loan from owner			1000.00	1000.00
9/29	302	Kyle Wayne	200.00	12.00		212.00
9/29	303	Cynthia Jones	250.00	15.03		265.53
	Total		63100.00	4389.00	10000.00	77489.00

If the company uses a cash register, the "log-out" total tape is posted to the cash receipts journal and the daily tapes are stored for future reference.

The sales journal and the cash receipts journal measure the same thing: income to the company. However, there are two important differences between them:

■ The sales journal contains only sales to customers, while the cash receipts journal includes non-business income sources such as loans and refunds.

■ The sales journal is a record of sales *at the time they are earned* while the cash receipts journal does not record the sales *until the cash is received*. For companies on the accrual basis, accountants enter a sale in the income statement when it is earned.

Purchase journal

The purchase journal is used to record goods and services used in the business. The journal shows the date, source, cost and description for every purchase.

A purchase journal has two purposes:

■ If the company purchases on credit (that is, when it receives goods or services but has not yet paid for them), the purchase journal allows the recording of expenses when they occur, rather than when they are paid.

■ The purchase journal is the source of information to keep track of accounts payable - amounts owed to suppliers.

An example of a purchase journal is found in Figure 7-4, below. The format of this journal varies considerably between companies, depending on the type and size of company and how the company manages its accounts payable.

figure 7-4

Example - Purchase Journal

Date	Supplier	Amount	Materials	Utilities	Repairs	Office	Legal Fee	Gasoline
9/01	Standard Materials Co.	1900.00	1900.00					
9/01	Rogers and Grant	1500.00					1500.00	
9/01	Bridgeport Hydraulic	750.00		750.00				
9/01	Hyde Stationers	75.00				75.00		
9/01	Visa Credit Card	170.00			75.00	15.00		80.00
9/30	Chamber of Commerce	150.00				150.00		
	Total	15200.00	7000.00	2000.00	700.00	245.00	3000.00	2255.00

A real-life purchase journal might have 20 or 30 columns: one each for the company's different expense categories. For many small businesses, this journal may not be necessary. That is because a small company may not have a large enough volume of credit purchases to justify the cost of the extra record-keeping. A small company will find that an accounts payable record does the job well enough. The company's CPA or business advisor can help with this decision.

The *accounts payable* record that links to the purchase journal resembles the customer accounts receivable record and works the same way. One record is kept for each supplier. Purchases are posted to the supplier's record, adding to the balance. When an invoice is paid, the payment is deducted from the supplier's balance. An example of an accounts payable ledger card is shown in Figure 7-5, on the next page.

figure 7-5

```
Example - Accounts payable ledger

    Supplier name        Standard Materials Company

    Date  Description       Purchase  Payment   Balance

    9/01  Balance forward                        800.00
    9/03  Paid invoice                 800.00       .00
    9/06  Widgets received  1900.00             1900.00
    9/10  Widgets received  1000.00             2900.00
    9/15  Widgets received  3000.00             4900.00
    9/17  Paid on account              3000.00  1900.00
    9/22  Widgets received   500.00             2400.00
    9/30  Paid on account              2000.00   400.00
```

Cash disbursements journal

Like the cash receipts journal, this journal must be maintained for every company. It records all the money the company pays out, regardless of the purpose. The journal records the date paid, who it was paid to, the check number, the amount and what it was for. The term *cash* does not refer to payments made with currency or dollar bills. Currency payments are normally recorded in the cash receipts journal because they are typically made out of the day's receipts. As with cash receipts, accuracy in this journal is critical.

The format of the cash disbursements journal is similar to that of the purchases journal. Both records must be able to identify the details of each transaction. This categorization is known as the *chart of accounts*, described later in this chapter.

Payroll journal

This journal gives essential details about payroll paid to employees. In addition to containing all the information to prepare W-2s for employees, it has vital information for insurance coverage and shows the amount of taxes withheld from employees' paychecks, which must be paid over to the Federal and state governments. Figure 7-6, on Page 7-8, is an example of a simple payroll journal.

figure 7-6

Example - Payroll journal						
Date Employee	Gross	Federal Tax	State Tax	FICA	Medical	Net Pay
9/15 Roger Prentiss	500.00	75.00	22.50	37.50	5.00	360.00
9/15 Jane Rogers	600.00	90.00	27.00	45.00	5.00	433.00
9/15 Cynthia Stafford	350.00	52.50	15.75	26.25	4.00	251.50
9/15 Anna O'Sullivan	245.00	36.75	11.00	19.00	3.00	175.25
9/15 Gary Shannon	700.00	105.00	31.50	52.50	5.00	506.00
Total	8000.00	1200.00	360.00	600.00	75.00	5765.00

For more information about payroll, refer to Chapter 8 - Payroll and Payroll Taxes for a complete discussion.

General journal

A general journal is used to record a few transactions that cannot be recorded in the special journals. Among these transactions are adjusting, closing and correcting entries. This journal is normally maintained by the company's CPA or bookkeeper.

PRACTICAL FORMS OF BUSINESS RECORDS

Each of the above journals can be purchased from business forms vendors. These companies sell standard records systems that can be customized for most companies. There are many publishers of these records, so it is only possible to mention the main categories.

Weekly or monthly accounting records

These systems are designed for very small businesses and are widely sold in stationery stores. The best known are published under the "Dome" name. They allow a small company to keep track of cash receipts and disbursements transactions. They are also portable; they are easily carried in a truck, car or briefcase, making it convenient to keep business records up-to-date. However, they are not practical for a company that sells on credit, because they don't provide a way to keep track of amounts owed by customers.

One write systems

A "one-write" system uses carbon strips or "carbonless" paper to record journal information at the same time that business documents are prepared. By writing the information once, company personnel save time and reduce errors in posting journals.

A one-write sales system is an example. When an invoice is prepared for a customer, the sales information is being posted to the sales journal and to the customer accounts receivable card at the same time. When payment is received, the data is posted to the bank deposit ticket, cash receipts journal and customer's account card - all at the same time.

The accounts payable one-write system is the most popular. When a check is prepared, it updates a disbursements journal and vendor record at the same time, through a carbon stripe on the back of the check. Other systems are available for purchase journals, payroll, inventory records and other applications.

Like the Weekly Accounting Records discussed above, the one-write system is convenient to carry around.

COMPUTER SYSTEMS

A computer is a practical way to keep the records for many small businesses. Of course, the cost of a computer is much higher than that of any other record-keeping system. But, the long-range cost is comparable, or even cheaper, for three reasons:

■   The computer records system saves on outside bookkeeping and accounting costs.
■   The computer system gives managers faster access to company information such as sales, customer receivables and supplier payables.
■   The computer system saves managers' time, allowing them to be more productive.

The key to an effective computer installation is the software. It must process the company's information, be easy to use, and be able to grow with the company without being so full-featured that employees are unable to learn to use it.

Small company owners should be practical about computer selection. It may not be a good idea to computerize a company in its first year of operation unless the computer is an indispensable aspect of its operations. Cost is not necessarily the drawback to computer systems for small start-up businesses. In fact, it is possible to purchase a powerful business-oriented computer system for under $2,500, including hardware and software. The real problems are the time it takes to implement a computer system and the possibility that the system may not be the right one for the company.

Pros and cons of computers

Pros:

- Computers can significantly decrease time needed to gather and organize information.

- Better information allows owners and managers to make better decisions.

- Computerization can save money on accounting fees.

- Once the accounting system is operating, owners and managers will get numbers much faster.

- Computerization combines many operations into one.

- Computerization may provide for increased profits and improved morale.

- Computerization may increase customer satisfaction.

Cons:

- Purchasing hardware and software requires forethought and planning.

- The initial purchase of software and hardware could be costly.

- Personnel must be trained on the new software.

- May confront resistance from personnel by converting to an automated accounting system.

Hardware selection

Once the decision to computerize has been made, the first thing to do is get a computer system. There are several terms that one must know before purchasing a system.

■ Central Processing Unit (CPU) - The main part of the computer system. It comes in various speeds, from 20 to 50 megahertz (MHz). The higher the number the faster the computer runs. In addition, most CPUs sold today are designated as 286, 386 or 486, with the 486 being more powerful. For small business computing a 386 running 25mhz is the minimum practical configuration.

■ Random-Access Memory (RAM) - The area of the computer where work is saved temporarily while computing takes place. A system usually comes equipped with 1 to 8 megabytes of RAM. For small business computing 4 megabytes of RAM is the minimum practical configuration.

■ Hard disk - The place to permanently store information. Common hard disk sizes range from 80 to 320 megabytes. For small business computing a 100 megabyte drive is the smallest practical size.

■ Disk Operating System (DOS) - The software that runs the computer. DOS controls what your computer is doing at all times. For small business computing MS-DOS is the preferred operating system.

Once familiar with the basic computer terms one must decide how powerful a system to purchase, and how much money to spend. The software programs mentioned later will all run on a 386 or 486, 2-4 megabytes of RAM and a hard disk of 120-200 megabytes.

A printer should be part of any computer system you own. Printers come in two common forms, dot-matrix and laser. Dot-matrix printers are inexpensive but lack in quality. Laser printers are more expensive but have superior quality. If the printer is to be used to fill in forms such as payroll tax forms then a dot-matrix is recommended.

A modem is a device used to transmit or receive information through a telephone line between computers. A modem is not necessary to run an accounting system, but it is useful if you work at home or require assistance from your accountant.

Software options

The first step is to research the software programs available. The market consists of hundreds of different systems. Three ways to narrow the field are to shop around, ask other small business owners what they are using and ask accountants what software they would recommend.

Most small startup companies can fill their needs with systems that sell for less than $200. Four of these full featured programs are discussed below.

One Write Plus (OWP)

This software is the computerized version of the manual "one write" system. For a bookkeeper who is familiar with the manual system, the conversion to the computerized system should be relatively simple. OWP comes with modules for Accounts Receivable (AR), Accounts Payable (AP), General Ledger (GL), Payroll (PR), Cash Disbursements (CD), and Cash Receipts (CR). OWP comes with an inventory control system and can print checks and customer invoices.

Peachtree

Like One-Write Plus, this package includes AR, AP, CD, CR and GL modules. Bank Reconciliation is included for free. The Payroll software is available but at an additional cost.

DacEasy Accounting

This inexpensive program includes AR, AP, CD, CR and GL. DacEasy offers package deals which allows users to purchase the basic package and to add Payroll, Inventory or Automated Cash Registers for a low price.

Quickbooks

Like One-Write Plus, this package includes AR, AP, CD, CR and GL modules. The Payroll software is available but at an additional cost.

The software listed above is sold through independent consultants, mail order and software retailers. The numbers are listed below:

One Write Plus:	1-800-523-2422	**Peach Tree:**	1-800-247-3224
DacEasy:	1-800-222-8778	**QuickBooks:**	1-800-624-8742

Support plans

Once a software package has been purchased, the user is given the option of purchasing any updates at a reduced price as soon as they are available to the public. These updates are the new software package on the market, with complete documentation. In some cases the annual updates are included in the original purchase price.

In addition, each software package includes phone numbers for technical support, help when installing, questions on the basics as well as advanced questions.

Making the decision

Choosing a software package should not be a casual decision. Before shopping around, list the functions which are necessary for the company and locate those software packages which fulfill your needs. Then, compare any special offers that might be included, cost of the original package, cost of updates, demands and limitations on the computer hardware and compatibility with other software. Once this is done the rest is easy. All that is left to do is read the manual and play around with the program to learn its idiosyncrasies.

Backing up computer data

The purpose of back-up is to give a solid starting place from which to recreate files. The easiest way to do this is to date your transaction batches and back-up disks. Back-ups should be stored off the premises in a fireproof container. This is a precaution if there is any loss of data on the computer. The back-up should be done daily.

Checklist of procedures

Daily:

- Generate bank deposits when entering cash receipts.

- Print cash receipts and cash disbursements.

- Post daily activity.

- Back-up onto floppy disk. Store back-ups in safe, separate locations.

Monthly:

- Print AR and AP aged trial balances.

- Perform bank reconciliations.

- Post adjusting entries.

- Print trial balances.

- Print monthly general ledger (current period only).

- Print monthly financial statements.

- Compare account balances to reconciliations.

- Back-up onto floppy disk. Store back-ups in safe, separate locations.

Yearly:

- Post final adjusting entries.

- Print final AR and AP aged trial balances.

- Print year-to-date GL.

- Make second copy of back-up.

- Store back-ups in safe, separate locations.

- Close year-end (after consulting accountant).

MANAGING AND SUMMARIZING INFORMATION

The system for keeping track of any business records consists of accounts. An account is the basic storage unit for accounting data. There is a separate account for each asset, liability, component of owner's equity, revenue and expense. The book which contains all the accounts is called the ledger. In order to be able to find an account in the ledger easily, the accounts are numbered. The account number tells both the location of the account and its financial statement classification. The list of numbers and the corresponding account names is called the *chart of accounts*.

The use of a chart of accounts facilitates analysis of business records and preparation of reports such as the balance sheet and income statement. Accountants use account numbers because they process the data by computer. Also, it makes it easier to put the information in order. For example, the balance sheet is the first report in the financial statements, followed by the income statement. The balance sheet always lists assets first then liabilities and owner's equity. The income statement shows revenues first then expenses.

A simple chart of accounts for a small company might use a three digit number for each account where the 100s are used for assets, the 200s for liabilities and owner's equity, the 300s for revenues and the 400s for expenses. Appendix U shows an example of a chart of accounts.

USING ACCOUNTING DATA TO MANAGE

The purpose of this section is to explain what the accounting professional does with the company records to turn them into financial statements. It is a basic explanation of two important financial statements. It also discusses how small company owners can use accounting data to estimate the company's income. Finally, it explains the significance of the accounting information. This discussion is not a substitute for a meeting with the company's accountant or financial advisor to learn to understand the statements and how to use the information to run the company and make business decisions.

The information from these journals is summarized and the totals are used to prepare financial statements and tax returns. Many company owners will prefer to turn the summarized records over to a CPA or other accounting professional to be processed into financial statements. Besides getting the job done, this allows the business manager to use the services of a professional to interpret the information while the owner concentrates on running the company.

Using either a computer system or paper-based techniques, the accountant accumulates the company data into another record called a *general ledger*. From the general ledger, all reports are prepared, including company financial statements, sales tax reports and income tax returns. This is the first document that tax examiners and auditors want to see when they look at the company's "books."

The chart in Figure 7-7 shows a simplified flow of data from basic documents to the end product.

figure 7-7

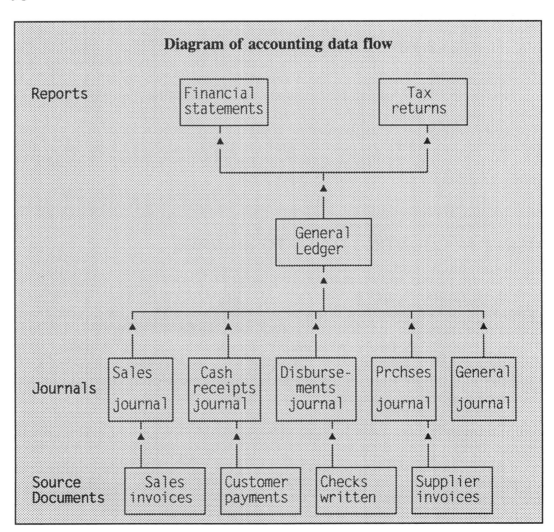

There are two main financial statements: the income statement and the balance sheet.

Income statement

This statement shows the components of profit or loss for a company. It can cover any period of time, from a month to a year, but never more than a year. Typical small businesses have an income statement prepared either quarterly, semi-annually or annually. Larger ones do so every month; That is because larger businesses find it harder, and riskier, to rely on personal observation to evaluate the company's financial success.

Figure 7-8, on Page 7-18, shows the annual income statement for a small manufacturing company. The statement shows, on the right side, the source of data for each line. In most cases, it is possible to get a *rough approximation* of the company's income by entering data from company accounting records. Appendix W contains a worksheet that can be used for this purpose. This worksheet will produce an estimated income statement, not a substitute for a professionally prepared income statement.

figure 7-8

Example - Income statement

Superior Widget Company
Statement of Income
For the year ended December 31, 1993

Sales		$ 100,000	A
Cost of goods sold			
Materials	30,000		B
Subcontract	15,000		B
Direct labor	6,000	51,000	C
Gross profit		49,000	
Operating expenses			
Salaries	25,000		C
Rent and utilities	5,000		B&D
Administrative	4,500		B&D
Marketing	3,500	38,000	B&D
Net income before taxes		11,000	
Federal and state income tax		4,750	E
Net income after taxes		$ 6,250	

Data sources:

    A.   Sales journal
    B.   Purchases journal
    C.   Payroll Journal
    D.   Cash disbursements journal
    E.   Estimated, based on current tax rules

Of course, the most important item on the income statement is the net income after taxes. Beyond that, however, the format of the income statement allows a fast analysis of company performance. Each main component of the statement has a meaning.

Comparison to prior periods or to a budget

To be truly useful, the income statement should have comparative figures to the previous year or to the company's budget. Few small businesses have formal budgets. Those that do, and use the budgets as goals, find it helps them to improve profitability. The simplest budget for any company expresses management's goals for sales and net profits. This two-factor target allows managers to make action plans to achieve the goals. If the goals are not met, corrective actions can be taken.

Cost of sales

Cost of sales is a term used to define the cost to produce, buy or modify the item being sold. Anything that is part of the product or touches the product directly is a part of the cost of sales. Any material used is the first and most obvious cost of sales as is the payroll of anyone involved in producing a product or providing a service. All expenses included in cost of sales vary directly with sales. That is, the more widgets that are sold or the more services performed, the greater the cost of sales.

Gross profit

Gross profit is the profit after cost of sales is subtracted from sales and before any other expenses are deducted. This figure is an important measure of profitability. To be successful, a company must sell its goods or services for enough above cost to pay operating expenses and make a profit.

Operating expenses

Operating expenses are costs, other than cost of sales, incurred in running a business. Whether one widget is sold or one hundred, these costs remain relatively the same. Some common examples are utilities, rent and office expense. Obviously, as sales increase, there comes a point when operating costs will increase but the relationship is not a direct one.

Net income before taxes

This number is significant because it is the amount that determines how much tax a company pays. Any state tax is an expense for federal tax purposes, but neither state nor federal taxes are allowed as expenses on the state income tax return.

Federal and state income tax

These are an expense of doing business and making a profit and are included as expenses in a company's financial statements.

Net income after taxes

This is the net increase in owner's equity resulting from a company's operations. Net income equals revenue less expenses.

Balance sheet

A balance sheet normally accompanies any professionally prepared income statement. It is also required for all financial statements requested by banks. The balance sheet is a report of the company's *assets* and *liabilities*. It also shows the amount of the owners' interest or *equity* in the company. The equity is the amount by which the assets exceed the liabilities.

The balance sheet is a snapshot at a specific moment in time of the assets the company owns, the amount it owes to others, and the amount of the owners' stake in the company. It shows the resources available to run the company, how much of those resources are already committed, how liquid the assets are and whether the liquid assets are adequate to pay the company's bills.

Figure 7-9, on Page 7-21, shows a balance sheet for a small manufacturing company. As with the income statement, it is possible to estimate the company's balance sheet from readily available information. Appendix V contains a worksheet that can be used for this purpose. Of course, this worksheet is not a substitute for a professionally prepared balance sheet.

figure 7-9

Example - Balance sheet

Superior Widget Company
Balance sheet
As of December 31, 1993

Assets

Current assets	
Cash	$ 5,000
Accounts receivable	6,250
Inventory	5,500
	16,750
Property & equipment	
Equipment	25,500
Vehicles	9,900
Furniture	2,600
	38,000
Less accumulated depreciation	30,000
	8,000
Total Assets	24,750

Liabilities and Shareholders' Equity

Current liabilities	
Accounts payable	6,250
Notes payable, current	4,750
Accrued expenses & taxes	1,000
	12,000
Other liabilities	
Notes payable, due after one year	4,000
Shareholders equity	
Common stock	1,000
Retained earnings	7,750
	8,750
Total liabilities & Shareholders' Equity	24,750

An important limitation of the balance sheet is that it uses historical values for assets. This means the assets are valued at what they cost, not what they are worth. This difference is most apparent for real estate and other assets that fluctuate in value. In times of rising real estate values, the company's real estate holdings may be worth more than they are valued on the company balance sheet.

However, traditional financial statements do not increase the values to the higher market values. If the difference is critical, the company should hire an appraiser to prepare a separate valuation of the company. This is usually only necessary when the company wants to borrow money.

HOW TO IMPROVE THE COMPANY'S RECORDS

Accountants know there can be a strong correlation between good records and good profits. Companies that keep good records seem to be more profitable than those that don't. Good records allow managers to: resolve customer billing questions; avoid double-paying bills; analyze selling prices and costs; withstand tax audits. This section offers suggestions on how to keep good company records. Appendix S is a summary of how long records should be kept.

Spend time on setup

Good records reduce accounting fees, so the money spent to set up good records returns as future cost savings. This is really a two step process. The first is to design the records system and put it into operation for one or two months. The second is to review the results of the trial operation and fine-tune record keeping formats and procedures.

Use a qualified trained bookkeeper

Whoever keeps company records, the owner, a spouse, employee or outside bookkeeper, should be properly trained and understand the importance of maintaining good records. Sources of this training include community college, bookkeeping seminars, the company's accountants and many others. Truly good bookkeepers are valuable; they make life easier for business owners and protect them from tax problems. Bookkeeping requires skills and discipline. A poorly trained bookkeeper or one who does not have the required skills could be very costly.

Keep records up to date

Financial information is useful only if it is timely. Each month should be treated as a separate business cycle and records should be up to date at the end of every month. Month end procedures should include totaling receipts and disbursements journals and balancing cash, accounts receivable, accounts payable and bank loans. Many small businesses cannot afford formal monthly financial statements. As a substitute, after monthly procedures, owners should review income and expenses. One tool to use is the month-end "closing checklist." This is a list of the things to do to complete the company's record-keeping at the end of the month. The company's CPA could help customize one for the company.

Organize records

The company's records consist of journals and the original documents that support them. This includes cash register tapes, customer invoices, bank statements, paid bills and canceled checks. These should be filed so they can retrieved quickly. Both the Internal Revenue Service and Connecticut law require these documents be retained for three years, if not longer. Appendix S is a checklist of how long various records must be retained.

Keep business and personal finances separated

Many business owners feel they can do whatever they please with the company funds and records. This is not necessarily true. In the eyes of the Internal Revenue Service, the bank and the courts, the company is a separate entity and the owners are required to keep an arms-length distance from it. The best way is for owners to treat their companies as if they were unrelated. Besides separate records, the money should be separate. Unless an expenditure is directly related to the company, it should be paid directly from the owners' personal checking accounts. If an expenditure is partly personal and partly business, the personal part should be paid from personal funds and the business portion paid from the company account. This separation reduces the potential for error, reduces bookkeeping time, saves on accounting fees and reduces audit problems with the IRS.

Understand and use available financial information

A regular review of company financial performance helps keep the company on track and avoid future problems. The two basic financial statements, income statement and balance sheet, were discussed in the previous section. They are the starting point for financial reviews. The form the two basic statements take and how often they're needed depend on the company size and other factors. The form can range from an approximation to CPA-prepared statements.

Don't ignore financial signals

It is difficult for the owners and founders of small businesses to look objectively at their creations. Good financial information allows that objective look. Too often, business owners ignore financial information when it shows mistakes in judgement. This carelessness can be costly. If the financial statements show a decision is wrong, recognize the error and correct it. The real measure of success is the long term prosperity and growth of the company. Mistakes along the way are learning tools and can contribute to the long term success of the company.

CONCLUSION

Good record keeping is essential to every company no matter what the size. Even the smallest company must prepare tax returns and be able to explain the numbers used if audited by the Internal Revenue Service. As a company grows, financial results must be known in order to manage the company successfully and to make business decisions based on reliable information.

Chapter 8
Payroll and Payroll Taxes

INTRODUCTION

Even if a company has only one employee, it must follow the same federal and state payroll regulations as employers with large payrolls.

Every Connecticut employer must withhold three taxes from all employees' pay: federal income taxes, state income taxes and Social Security taxes. The employer must deposit these withheld taxes with Federal and State collectors promptly. These funds are the personal responsibility of the employer's owners and managers. If they are not deposited, the government can seek payment directly from the owners and managers. Besides taxes withheld from employees' pay, the employer must also pay, from its own funds, social security taxes, federal unemployment taxes and state unemployment taxes.

ORGANIZATION OF CHAPTER

This chapter covers these important aspects of payroll:

Payroll record keeping
Federal payroll taxes
Federal payroll tax deposits
Connecticut payroll taxes
Connecticut payroll tax deposits
Employee versus independent contractor
Forms required from employees
Registration forms required for employers
Recurring payroll reports
Payroll decisions and policies

PAYROLL RECORD KEEPING

Payroll is one of the company's most demanding record keeping tasks. These records include details of hours worked, taxes withheld and payments made. The company must report summary information to tax collectors every quarter and submit detailed information once each year. Many small companies find it tempting to ignore these numerous, costly and complex procedures. By doing so, they face equally costly penalties.

There are two types of payroll records: basic employee information and earnings information. Basic employee information includes the following:

- Name.
- Address.
- Sex.
- Date of birth.
- Social security number.
- Withholding exemptions.
- Occupation.
- Period employed.
- State employed in.
- Pay rate and history of raises.

Many employers make the mistake of asking for this information on an application form. Federal discrimination laws make it illegal for employers to ask for any personal information that would disclose an applicant's ethnic, racial or religious background. This information is best gathered *after* the employee is hired. The personal information is normally kept in a file folder for each employee. The file would also contain the employee's application, performance evaluations, reprimands, health insurance data and similar information.

Earnings information includes all the data needed for payment calculations and to prepare government reports. The company must keep a record, for each payroll period, of the following information about each employee's earnings:

- Gross wages paid.
- Federal income tax withheld.
- State income tax withheld.
- Social Security and Medicare taxes withheld.
- Fringe benefits withheld.
- Net wages paid.

If the employee is paid by the hour, the employer must also keep a record of this information:

■   Hours worked.
■   Overtime hours worked.

Although it is not required, it is a good idea to report this information to the employee with each paycheck.

This information must be summarized each quarter and at the end of the year for government reports of wages, taxes and withholding. Records of employment taxes must be retained for at least four years and be available for Internal Revenue Service review (see appendix S for specifics). These should include all copies of returns filed along with dates and amounts of tax deposits made. The detailed records of hours, payments and withholdings should be kept for three years. Connecticut only requires employers to keep records for three years.

There are several ways to maintain this earnings information, and the company is free to use whatever records it wants as long as they are accurate and complete. There are four main alternatives: individual record cards, payroll books, computer and payroll services.

Individual record card

This is a paper record, usually 5" x 8" or 8½" x 11", that records every paycheck paid to the employee during the year. It is subtotaled at the end of each calendar quarter and totaled at the end of the year. These subtotals and totals allow the company to prepare quarterly reports of taxes and unemployment insurance. Payroll record cards can be purchased from stationery stores and one-write vendors. If the company uses a "one write" system, discussed in Chapter 7, the payroll record card is filled out at the same time as the paycheck is written.

Payroll book

These books are sold in stationery stores and allow the company to summarize both employee information and company payroll figures. A popular brand is the DOME payroll book which is available through department stores and most stationery retailers.

Computer

If the company already has a computer, it may find it economical to purchase a payroll program to prepare payments, government reports and accounting summaries. Because payroll requirements change almost every year, the company usually has to purchase an update every year.

Payroll preparation services

Several independent service bureaus sell payroll preparation services. The payroll service keeps all records for the company, including employee data and earnings information. With most payroll services, the company calls in its payroll information. The service prepares the checks and returns them to the employer before payday.

Payroll services also prepare all government reports, including quarterly tax reports and annual W-2 forms, and will automatically prepare tax deposit checks when needed. Other features include specialized accounting reports and direct deposit of earnings into employees' bank accounts.

Many small business owners prefer to use payroll services in order to relieve themselves of record keeping responsibilities and also of the need to keep track of changes in payroll laws. This gives them more time to spend running their businesses. Appendix M lists the major payroll preparation services in Connecticut. The company's CPA firm may also be a source for payroll or payroll report preparation.

FEDERAL PAYROLL TAXES

Federal payroll taxes fall into three categories:

- Federal income tax withholding taxes paid by the employee.

- Social Security and Medicare taxes (FICA - Federal Insurance Contributions Act) paid by the employee with matching contributions by the employer.

■ Federal Unemployment taxes (FUTA - Federal Unemployment Tax Act) paid by the employer only.

Details on all three types of taxes are found in the Internal Revenue Service Employer's Tax Guide (Circular E). This publication is automatically sent to all companies that have employees. It may also be obtained by mail or phone from the IRS. See Appendix J for current addresses and toll-free numbers.

Federal income tax withholding is calculated on individual employee data (wages, marital status, exemptions, and frequency of payroll). Commonly used tax tables are listed in Circular E.

Employee wages subject to federal income tax withholding include all pay rendered for services performed. This can be in the form of salaries, vacation pay, sick pay, bonuses, and commissions. Employee wages may be in the form of cash or other sources. There is no limit to the amount of wages subject to withholding taxes.

Employees may also be compensated in the form of fringe benefits. A fringe benefit is anything of value given to employees in addition to their salary or wages. There are taxable fringe benefits, the value of which must be added to the employee's gross earnings to be taxed for federal, FICA, and unemployment taxes. Some examples of this are employer-provided cars, prizes, memberships in country clubs, airfare, vacations, tickets to entertainment or sporting events. Circular E contains a complete list of the items that are taxable.

There are also non-taxable fringe benefits which can be given to employees and are not included in their earnings. Some examples are: qualified employee discounts on company products, working condition fringes, employer provided meals and on-site athletic facilities.

Federal Insurance Contributions Act withholdings, or FICA, consists of two component parts - Social Security and Medicare, using different wage bases for each component. The rates and wage bases change every year, usually increasing a small amount each year. The changes take place on January 1 each year, and are published in IRS Circular E. When the Circular E arrives, company managers should study it for possible changes in tax withholding.

The table in Figure 8-1, on Page 8-6, is an example of the calculation for 1994.

The employer's matching contribution is calculated using the same rates and wage bases. Thus, in 1994, for an employee who earns $70,000, the *total* tax paid would be 15.3% of earnings up to $60,600 for social security and medicare and an extra 2.9% of earnings over $60,600 for medicare alone. Each part is figured as shown in Figure 8-1 below.

figure 8-1

```
┌────────────────────────────────────────────────────────────────┐
│           Example - Analysis of 1994 FICA and Medicare          │
│            payments for an employee earning $70,000             │
│                                                                 │
│   Wage base          Rate      Employer Share    Employee Share │
│   Up to $60,600      7.65%    $     4,635.90    $     4,635.90   │
│   over $60,600       1.45%          136.30            136.30     │
│                                                                 │
│   Total                      $     4,772.20    $     4,772.20    │
│                                                                 │
│                                                                 │
│       The 7.65% rate consists of two separate components:       │
│                                                                 │
│   Social Security Tax                                  6.20%     │
│   Medicare Tax                                         1.45%     │
│                                                                 │
│   Total                                               7.65%     │
└────────────────────────────────────────────────────────────────┘
```

Federal Unemployment Taxes (FUTA) are calculated at the rate of 6.2% on the first $7,000 of gross wages paid to each employee. In figuring FUTA tax, the employer can deduct a maximum credit of up to 5.4% for state unemployment taxes paid, resulting in a net federal unemployment tax of 0.8%. (See Federal Payment section.) The current percentages and gross wage limits are found in IRS Circular E and should be verified annually.

FEDERAL PAYROLL TAX DEPOSITS

There are two recurring federal tax payments: 1) federal withholding and FICA taxes combined into a single payment known as a "Federal 941" deposit, and 2) FUTA payment, known as a "Federal 940" deposit.

Federal 941 Deposits

Federal payroll taxes must be deposited according to the frequency assigned each company by the IRS. Each November the IRS advises businesses what their deposit status is for the following year. This deposit schedule is based on taxes reported on Federal 941s during a four-quarter "lookback" period - July 1 through June 30, illustrated in the chart below. If a company reported employment taxes of $50,000 or less during this lookback period, it becomes a **monthly** depositor; if a company reported more than $50,000 during this period it becomes a **semi-weekly** depositor. There are two exceptions to these rules, the $500 depositor and the $100,000 depositor.

figure 8-2

EXAMPLE: Lookback period for calendar year 1994		
If you deposited:		
	Example 1	Example 2
Jul - Sep 1992	2,500	20,000
Oct - Dec 1992	2,500	20,000
Jan - Mar 1993	2,500	20,000
Apr - Jun 1993	2,500	20,000
Your total deposits were	10,000	80,000
Your 1994 deposit schedule	Monthly	Semi-weekly

New employers are generally monthly depositors for the first year of business.

The table in Figure 8-3, on Page 8-8, shows the requirements for making 941 tax deposits.

figure 8-3

Deposit requirements for payroll taxes	
Deposit Rule	Deposit Due
QUARTERLY RULE	
If at the end of the quarter your total tax liability is less than $500:	You may pay the taxes to the IRS with your Form 941 quarterly return, or you may deposit them by the due date of the return.
MONTHLY RULE	
If your total tax liability during the "lookback" period was $50,000 or less:	You must deposit the taxes accumulated in any month by the 15th of the following month, so long as your total tax obligation is at least $500 but not more than $100,000 (see one-day rule below).
SEMI-WEEKLY RULE	
If your total tax liability during the "lookback" period was more than $50,000:	Taxes accumulated for paydates of Wednesday through Friday must be deposited by the following Wednesday. Taxes accumulated for paydates of Saturday through Tuesday must be deposited by the following Friday.
$100,000 ONE-DAY RULE	
If your total accumulated tax reaches $100,000 or more on any day during a deposit period:	Taxes must be deposited by the next banking day whether an employer is a monthly or semiweekly depositor. If a monthly depositor accumulates $100,000 on any day it then becomes a semi-weekly depositor for the remainder of the calendar year and for the following calendar year.

FUTA deposits

The 940 FUTA tax for each quarter must be paid on or before the last day of the calendar month following each quarter. There is an exception - if the tax liability is less than $100.00, it is not necessary to make a deposit. That liability can be carried over to the next quarter.

To calculate its FUTA due for each quarter, the company multiplies its total gross wages subject to FUTA times .008. For example, if the total wages subject to FUTA were $21,000, the deposit amount would be $168.00: $21,000 times .008 equals $168.00.

Deposit coupons

Federal deposits for both 940 and 941 taxes are made using Form 8109 coupons provided by the Internal Revenue Service in booklet form. Complete the coupon following the instructions in the booklet. The deposit is made at any authorized depository bank or Federal Reserve bank. It must be accompanied by a completed Form 8109 coupon to insure proper credit to the company's account.

The bank will provide a receipt for tax deposits. This is an important record to retain to prove when the deposit was made and how much was deposited. *The IRS takes up to three years to complete its audit of tax deposits, so tax receipts and canceled checks should be kept at least that long.*

If the Form 8109 coupon is filled out incorrectly, the company will not get proper credit for its tax deposits. The result is a long process to straighten out the company's deposit account. The important information items in the coupon are the type of tax and tax period.

Federal deposit penalties

The Internal Revenue Service has the power to charge penalties for late tax deposits or for shortages in deposits. These penalties are very high. They range from 2% for deposits made one to five days after the due date to 15% for amounts not paid by the 10th day after the first delinquency notice. In addition to penalties, the IRS charges interest at ½% per month from the date of the return to the date the tax is paid. The maximum interest payable is 25% of the tax deposit.

Tax deposits are a serious matter. Employers should give tax deposits priority above all other payments for two reasons:

- The deposits are the personal responsibility of business owners and managers.

- Penalties and interest can cost an additional 40% of the original tax due.

CONNECTICUT PAYROLL TAXES

There are two forms of Connecticut state payroll taxes:

- State income taxes paid by employees.

- State unemployment taxes paid by employers.

Connecticut's *state income tax* became effective for payroll paid after October 1, 1991. The employer must withhold state income tax from all employees who are working in Connecticut. Like the federal income tax, there is a different rate for different types of taxpayers. The withholding rates and amounts are found in Connecticut Circular CT.

State unemployment tax is paid by the employer. The tax is calculated on the first $9,000 of gross wages for each employee using the contribution rate assigned by the state. Every employer has a different rate. When the company first registers, it is given a tentative contribution rate. This rate changes every March and can move up or down based upon the amount of unemployment claims filed against the company. The taxable wage base is also subject to change, and is scheduled to increase to $15,000 by 1999.

CONNECTICUT PAYROLL TAX DEPOSITS

The two different state tax payroll payments go to two different state agencies on two different forms.

Income taxes

These deposits are made with a coupon similar to that for the Federal withholding taxes: Connecticut Form CT-WH. Employers must deposit state taxes with the same frequency as for payments to the Internal Revenue Service. Whenever the company reaches the point at which a Federal payment is required, it must make a state payment, regardless of the amount that has been withheld. Presently, the deposit coupon and accompanying payment are mailed to the Connecticut Department of Revenue Services.

Unemployment taxes

The state unemployment tax due is reported and paid quarterly with Form UC-2 within one month after the end of each calendar quarter. The tax is calculated and remitted with the form. This tax is deposited with the Connecticut Department of Labor.

EMPLOYEE VERSUS INDEPENDENT CONTRACTOR

One important aspect of managing a payroll is determining whether a worker is to be considered an employee or an independent contractor. This distinction affects tax payments:

■ If an employer-employee relationship exists, the employer must withhold federal and state income, and FICA tax, pay federal and state unemployment taxes and meet federal and state requirements on wages and hours.

■ If the worker is an independent contractor, the employer is relieved of all tax responsibilities. The worker is responsible for all taxes. In addition, the company does not have to pay workers' compensation and other employee benefits costs.

By definition, an employee is one who is paid to work under the direct control of the company. An independent contractor is someone who is hired to do a specific job and the one doing the hiring has no right to control the way the job is done. The independent contractor is generally paid a lump sum after the job is completed.

The employer should make a careful analysis to ensure the correct classification of all workers. It is tempting to classify employees as independent contractors to save on taxes. But, if they are later found to be employees, the employer faces severe penalties and interest and may have to use company funds to pay taxes that could have been withheld from employees' wages.

If an employer unintentionally disregards the withholding requirements for an employee, the penalty rate is 20% plus the original tax due. If the withholding rules are intentionally disregarded, the penalty rates are doubled. In addition, state and federal unemployment taxes would also be collected along with the penalties and interest assessed on those amounts.

The Internal Revenue Service has established "common-law" guidelines to be used in determining the status of workers. Figure 8-4 on Page 8-13 lists the factors the IRS takes into consideration in determining the relationship of a worker to the company. The factors are somewhat subjective, but if several of them apply, the worker could be considered to be an employee and not an independent contractor.

The IRS has a procedure for determining, in advance, whether a worker is an employee or independent contractor.

The company can get this determination by filing Form SS-8, which asks for the details of the worker's relationship to the company.

figure 8-4

IRS guidelines to determine if someone is an employee

1. The worker must comply with instructions on when, where and/or how a job must be done.

2. The worker is subject to periodic training.

3. The services of the worker are adapted to the continuing operation of the business.

4. Services are rendered personally by the worker, and thus do not permit substitute labor.

5. If the worker has the capacity to hire, supervise and pay others at the employer's direction the employee is considered to be acting as a representative of the company.

6. The worker enjoys a continuing relationship with the employer indicating a permanent relationship.

7. The worker has set hours to perform a job thus limiting freedom to come and go.

8. The worker is full time.

9. The worker performs the job on the employer's premises.

10. Services are performed according to a sequence set by the employer.

11. The worker is expected to submit periodic oral or written reports.

12. Payment is made by the hour, week or month rather than by a lump sum for a particular job.

13. The worker is reimbursed for travel and business expenses.

14. Tools and materials necessary to complete the job are furnished by the employer.

15. The worker does not maintain a substantial investment in the employer's premises.

16. The worker does not realize a personal profit or loss from the performance of the job.

17. The worker does not work for more than one firm at a time.

18. The worker's services are not available to the general public or other employers.

19. The employer has the right to fire the worker.

20. The employer does not have the right to terminate the relationship without incurring a liability.

FORMS REQUIRED FROM EMPLOYEES

The employer must obtain three forms from every employee:

- IRS form W-4.

- Connecticut Form CT-W4.

- Immigration and Naturalization Form I-9.

The *Employee's Withholding Allowance Certificate (Form W-4)* may be obtained from the local Internal Revenue Service office, by calling the IRS toll free number, from the company's CPA or from the company's payroll service. This form must be retained in each employee's personnel file. The W-4 provides the basic information required for payroll calculations: employee name, address, social security number, marital status and tax exemptions. If the employee chooses no withholding, the employer must send a copy of the W-4 form to the IRS.

The *Connecticut Employee Withholding Allowance Certificate Form (CT-W4)* is similar to that for the IRS. If the employee chooses no withholding, the employer doesn't have to withhold and doesn't have to send the form to the State.

The *Employment Eligibility Verification Form (Form I-9)* applies to every employee hired after November 6, 1986. Failure to comply may result in civil fines of from $100 to over $1,000. The I-9 and a booklet explaining how to use it may be obtained by calling the Immigration and Naturalization Service toll free number. This form must also be filed in the employee records.

REGISTRATION FORMS REQUIRED FOR EMPLOYERS

In order to make payroll payments, every employer must register for identification numbers with several government agencies. These are required for all employers, regardless of the form of business organization. Chapter 5, Small Business Legal Organization, contains a full description of the forms.

Three numbers are necessary for payroll payment:

■   Federal Employer Number - IRS Form SS-4.

■   Connecticut Identification number - Connecticut Form REG-1.

■   State Unemployment Tax Registration Number - Form UC-1A.

After the company has received its Federal, State and Unemployment Identification numbers, it will automatically receive the necessary quarterly and annual forms and information booklets that it needs to administer payroll. It must then file regular reports, as discussed in the next section.

RECURRING PAYROLL REPORTS

Quarterly reports

For reporting purposes, the year is divided into four quarters:

First quarter	January 1 through March 31
Second quarter	April 1 through June 30
Third quarter	July 1 through September 30
Forth quarter	October 1 through December 31

At the end of every quarter, three payroll reports are required. All are due on or before the last day of the month following the calendar quarter.

IRS Form 941

This is the reconciliation of federal income tax withholding, FICA withholding and federal deposits.

Connecticut Form CT-941

This is a quarterly reconciliation form similar to the IRS Form 941.

Connecticut Forms UC-2 and UC5A

These reports are combined on the same form. Form UC-2 reports the company's unemployment taxes and Form UC5A reports the wages paid to each employee. UC5A lists each employee's name, Social Security number and gross wages paid for the quarter. The state requires companies with 250 or more employees to submit this information via an acceptable magnetic tape or disk.

Annual reports

Every January and February are active months for employers. Besides the normal quarterly reports, they must furnish employees, the IRS and the State with detailed information statements. There are three annual reports:

- Federal Form 940.

- Federal Forms W-2 and W-3.

- Connecticut Form CT-W3.

The federal unemployment report, Form 940, must be completed and filed annually by January 31 following the close of the calendar year for which the tax is due.

The Wage and Tax Statement (Form W-2) must be sent by the end of January to each employee who was paid wages at any time during the year. A Transmittal of Income and Tax Statements (Form W-3), along with copies of all W-2s goes to the Social Security Administration by the end of February. If an employer issues 250 or more W-2s in a year, this information must be submitted to the Social Security Administration on a pre-approved tape or disk rather than by filing the hard paper copy. There is a penalty charge of $50.00 per individual form for failure to do this.

Connecticut requires an annual reconciliation form (CT-W3) reporting wages paid and taxes withheld. It also requires that the employer provide each employee with a wage and tax statement by January 31 of each year showing the amount of Connecticut income tax withheld for the prior year. This information can be shown on the federal W-2 and is acceptable by the state.

Information on how to prepare and file these annual reports, along with subcontractor miscellaneous income reports (1099 and 1096), can be found in the Circular E, or by calling the company's CPA or payroll processor.

Good records make the recurring tax deposits and reports a simple transfer of data. Failure to keep accurate records or make timely deposits may result in substantial penalties.

PAYROLL DECISIONS AND POLICIES

When setting up the payroll system, make it work for you by incorporating as many elements into the process as possible. Some questions you might ask are: should you pay weekly, bi-weekly, semi-monthly or monthly; will it be best to process the payroll in house or use an outside service; would you and your employees benefit by using electronic funds transfer thereby reducing costs and errors?

How to determine policy regarding hours, (i.e. regular and overtime) and salaried versus non-salaried employees hinges upon whether or not an employee is considered to be exempt rather than non-exempt from the Federal Fair Labor Standards Act. This act determines minimum and overtime wages depending on their assigned duties and responsibilities. Employees who are exempt from the Federal Fair Labor Standards Act regarding both minimum wage and overtime pay are categorized as legitimate administrators, executives, professional employees and outside salespeople. The rule in Figure 8-5 on Page 8-18 spell out the qualifications for exemption from minimum wage and overtime pay.

figure 8-5

Exemption Rules
1. Must do non-manual supervisory work.
2. Must regularly exercise discretion and independent judgment, free from immediate supervision in significant matters.
3. Must be an administrator who regularly assists an executive or perform specialized technical tasks.
4. Must have the authority to hire, fire or to recommend hiring and firing.
5. Must supervise two or more people.
6. Must not devote more than 20% (40% in retail or service establishments) of the employee's time to activities which may be considered non-exempt.
7. Must be paid at least $155 per week on a salary basis.
8. To be considered a professional, the employee's duties must involve work requiring knowledge of an advanced type or work that is original, creative, and primarily intellectual in nature.
9. To qualify for the exemption on the basis of being an outside salesperson, the employee must be one who makes sales at the customer's place of business rather than from the employer's base of operation.

An employee who qualifies as nonexempt under these rules must be paid in accordance with the Connecticut General Statutes regulating wages and hours. According to the statutes, *nonexempt* employees must be paid their wages weekly on a regular payday designated in advance. Payment may be held over 8 days, but if the regular payday falls on a non-work day, payment must be made on the preceding workday. A worker who is fired must be paid in full by the next business day. A worker who quits must be paid by the next regular payday, through regular payment channels or by mail. A worker who is laid off must be paid in full by the next regular payday.

In addition, the statutes regulate the method of payment. This may be done by cash, negotiable check, or upon an employee's written request, by a credit to the employee's account in any bank which has agreed with the employer to accept wage deposits (direct deposit). The employer must furnish each employee with each wage payment a record of hours worked, gross earnings with separate entries for straight time and overtime, itemized deductions, and net earnings. Exempt employees need not be shown a breakdown of hours and earnings.

At the time of hiring, the employee must be informed, in writing, of the rate of pay, hours, and wage payment schedule.

Employees must be notified in writing of changes in employment policies and also changes regarding wages, vacation pay, sick leave, health and welfare benefits, and related matters.

All nonexempt employees must be paid at least minimum wage. The Connecticut minimum wage is set at least at ½% more than the federal rate. Appendix R lists the current minimum wage rate. This covers the majority of the work force, but there are a few exceptions.

Tips

The most notable of these exceptions is for tipped employees in the restaurant and hotel industry. For these workers an hourly credit of up to 23% of minimum wage can be allowed under the assumption that tips earned will bring the employee's hourly rate to at least minimum wage. This "tip credit" is defined as the difference between minimum wage and the hourly wage paid to a tipped employee.

If an employer pays wages below minimum to a tipped employee, the employer is liable for FICA tax on the wages paid below the minimum wage and on the "deemed tips" (tip credit) that is used to make up the difference between the wages paid and the minimum wage.

> *EXAMPLE:*
>
> Assume a 23% tip credit and $4.27 minimum wage. Multiplying the minimum wage by 23% gives a 98 cent tip credit. The employer is allowed to pay this amount below minimum wage, assuming that the employee will make up the difference in tips, ($4.27 - .98 = 3.29). However, the employer is responsible for the FICA on the 98 cents in addition to the FICA on the $3.29.

Payment for overtime work

Overtime at the rate of time-and-one-half of the employee's regular rate must be paid after 40 hours work in a 7-day period. There is nothing in the federal or state wage-hour law that requires an employer to pay overtime after eight hours in a single day or for working weekends or holidays. However, overtime must be paid once a total of 40 hours is reached in any 7 day work week. An employee who works 30 hours one week and 50 the next, must be paid 10 hours at time and one half for the 50-hour week. Averaging is not permitted.

There are exceptions to the minimum wage and overtime regulations which affect certain employees in specific occupations (such as restaurant, hospital or farm workers). If there are doubts or questions concerning employees it is best to clarify this with the state labor commission. Failure to comply with the law can result in substantial penalties and back payments to employees should an audit indicate incorrect payments were made.

Other policies

Company policy varies from business to business and it is usually these individual policies which determine the answer to the following questions: how will vacation, holiday and sick time be allocated and how will they be tracked; what hours constitute the work day and work week; what benefits are available and how is eligibility determined; what is the frequency and rate of commission and bonus checks. A copy of this policy should be made available to each employee along with revisions when made.

Give serious consideration to the use of payroll deductions as a way to reduce the number of money transactions with an employee. Some of the more common deductions used are the employee portions of insurance benefits, savings plans, repayment of employee loans, garnishment payments, contributions to a flexible benefit plan, pension plan contributions, uniforms, union dues, and employee purchases. Another area for consideration is the inclusion of reimbursement of certain employee expenses such as mileage or travel expense.

CONCLUSION

Because the ease and accuracy of payroll management depends on good records, enough time is needed to manage the records properly. This means providing a safety margin of at least three to five days between the last day of the payroll period ending day and the actual payday. For example, if the payroll period ends on Friday, the payday should be on the following Wednesday or Friday.

Some new employers use the same date for both payroll period ending date and pay date. While this may work well initially, it becomes unmanageable as the company grows. Plan ahead and communicate with the employees.

INTRODUCTION

Tax planning is an important part of every company's business planning. The goal of tax planning is to pay the right amount of tax: not too much and not too little. The first step in tax planning is to select the correct form of business organization from the five options. The next step is to understand tax regulations and consider the tax results of business decisions. The third step is to keep good business records.

This chapter covers the second step: regulations and results. The tax consequences of many business actions depend on the form of business organization: sole proprietorship, partnership, limited liability company, "S" corporation or "C" corporation. Therefore, the chapter was designed to be read selectively. This is so readers can see the material for their type of business organization in one place and not have to read through material for other types of organization.

ORGANIZATION OF CHAPTER

Sole proprietorships
Partnerships
Limited liability companies
"C" corporations
"S" corporations
Calculating net income
Tax computation, credits and other taxes
Other tax considerations
Estimated taxes

SOLE PROPRIETORSHIPS

Net income taxed at individual level

The net income of a sole proprietorship is included in the individual federal income tax return of its owner. The gross income and allowable deductions are shown on Schedule C (Form 1040), Profit or Loss from Business. Once the net income has been computed on Schedule C, it is included with the owner's other tax information (i.e., wages, interest, etc.) to determine the owner's tax liability.

Assets of a Sole Proprietorship

A sole proprietorship has no existence apart from its owner. As a result, each asset in a sole proprietorship is treated as a separate business asset of the individual owner for federal income tax purposes.

Withdrawals from a Sole Proprietorship

If a company operates as a sole proprietorship, the owner doesn't receive a salary, so no federal income tax is withheld when the owner takes money out of the business. Instead, the owner takes a *draw*. The company sets up a *drawing account* on its books to keep track of the money the owner takes out. This account should identify money withdrawn for personal use to separate it from money paid for business expenses. There is no tax effect when the owner transfers money into, or out of, the business.

Because there is no tax withholding from draws, the owner must be sure to make quarterly tax payments to the IRS and Connecticut's Department of Revenue Services. These are discussed below under *Estimated Taxes*.

Federal Self-Employment Taxes

If the net income of a sole proprietorship is $400 or more, self-employment taxes will have to be paid in addition to regular taxes. Proprietors do not have to pay social security tax; the self-employment tax is the proprietor's form of Social Security tax. Thus, the rate is linked to the Social Security tax rate. The tax is figured on Schedule SE (Form 1040), Computation of Social Security Self-Employment Tax. Beginning in 1990, proprietors can deduct half of their self-employment income tax on their personal income tax forms.

Appendix R lists the current rates for self-employment tax.

State Income Taxes

The proprietor's taxable income for Connecticut is the same as that for the federal income tax. This amount is reported on Form CT-1040, Connecticut Individual Income Tax Return, and is included with the proprietor's other income, such as wages, interest and dividends, just like the IRS form 1040. If the proprietor loses money for the year, that loss can be deducted from the proprietor's other income. Connecticut does not have a separate self-employment tax, but, like the IRS, it requires proprietors to make estimated tax payments, discussed later in the chapter.

A Connecticut proprietor has no other filing requirements with the state. This makes it a much simpler form of business than partnerships and corporations.

Figure 9-1, below, summarizes the proprietor's income tax obligations. In addition, the sole proprietor must collect and pay the same payroll, excise and sales taxes as any other business owner. A full list appears in Appendix D.

figure 9-1

Income Tax Checklist for a Sole Proprietorship		
Type of Tax **Federal Taxes:**	Form Required	Due Date
Income Tax	Schedule C (Form 1040)	Same as Form 1040 (April 15th for calendar year individuals).
Self-Employment Tax	Schedule SE (Form 1040)	Same as Form 1040.
Estimated Tax	1040-ES	15th day of 4th, 6th and 9th months of tax years and 15th day of 1st month after the end of tax year.
State Taxes:		
Income Tax	CT-1040	Same as federal.
Self-Employment Tax	Not applicable	Not applicable.
Estimated Tax	CT-1040ES	Same as federal.

PARTNERSHIPS

Not a Taxable Entity - Net Income Taxed at Partner Level

A partnership is not a taxable entity. A separate U.S. Partnership Return of Income (Form 1065) is filed, but no tax is paid. The information from this return is used by the partners to prepare their personal tax returns. Thus, each partner's share of partnership net income (or loss) is taxed at the individual level. Figure 9-2, on Page 9-7, summarizes the partnership's tax obligations. A full list appears in Appendix E.

Allocation of Net Income to Partners

In determining their individual income tax liability for a year, partners must include their share of partnership income, whether or not it is actually paid out to them. This income is reported to the partners on Schedule K-1.

A partner's distributive share of partnership income is normally computed as described in the partnership agreement. This allocation of partnership income can become complicated, but for most small business partnerships, the income is divided by predefined shares. If there is an ownership change during a tax year, the income has to be apportioned accordingly.

Self-Employment Tax

A partner's share of partnership income is considered self-employment income. As a result, the partners pay self-employment taxes on their share of partnership income if their share is $400 or more. Partners do not have to pay social security tax; the self-employment tax is the partner's form of Social Security tax. Thus, the rate is linked to the Social Security tax rate. The tax is figured on Schedule SE (Form 1040), Computation of Social Security Self-Employment Tax. Beginning in 1990, partners can deduct half of their self-employment income tax on their personal income tax forms.

Appendix R lists the current rates for self-employment tax.

Assets of a Partnership

Generally, neither the partners nor the partnership recognize gain or loss when assets are contributed to a partnership. This general rule applies whether the partnership is just being formed or is already operating. Once assets have been contributed to a partnership, they are considered partnership assets for federal income tax purposes.

Partner's Basis in a Partnership

Partners must keep track of their *basis* in a partnership for several reasons. One reason is that the *basis* represents the limit of partnership losses that a partner may deduct on a personal tax return. Another is that a partner must pay capital gains tax on any distribution of property that exceeds the partner's *basis*.

A partner's original basis in a partnership equals the money and property the partner contributes to the partnership. The partner's basis is then increased by any partnership liabilities the partner assumes and decreased by any of the partner's personal liabilities assumed by the partnership. After the partnership begins operating, the partner's basis is continually adjusted.

The original basis is increased by:

■ Additional contributions to the partnership.
■ The partner's share of partnership income.
■ An increase in the partner's share of partnership liabilities.

The original basis is decreased (but not below zero) by:

■ Money and property distributed to the partner.
■ The partner's share of partnership losses.
■ A decrease in the partner's share of partnership liabilities.

Generally, if a partner contributes property other than cash to a partnership, the partnership's basis in that property is the same as the partner's basis in the property. The partnership then uses this basis in its accounting records for figuring depreciation and capital gains.

Once a partner's basis has been reduced to zero, any remaining partnership losses are postponed until such time as the partner has enough basis to absorb the postponed losses.

Withdrawals from a Partnership

When a partner withdraws cash from a partnership, there is no taxable gain unless the withdrawal is more than the partner's basis in the partnership. Thus, a partner's withdrawal of the original investment normally isn't taxable. Neither is withdrawal of the current year's income, even if the withdrawal takes place earlier in the year than the income is actually earned. These become taxable only if they exceed the partners' basis in the partnership.

If a partnership distributes property other than cash to a partner, there is generally no gain or loss to either the partner or the partnership. Instead, the partner takes the property with the same basis that the partnership had in the property.

State Income Taxes

Connecticut taxes a partner's share of partnership net income at the partner level. The taxable net income is the same amount as taxed for federal purposes. This amount is reported on Form CT-1040, Connecticut Individual Income Tax Return. Individual partners must make estimated tax payments throughout the year on Form CT-1040ES.

Connecticut, like the IRS, requires a partnership information form. This Form, CT-1065, reports financial and partner information but requires no tax payment, because the partners include the income on their personal returns.

LIMITED LIABILITY COMPANIES

A Limited Liability Company (LLC) is a new form of business entity recognized by the IRS and Connecticut. Essentially, it is an entity that combines the tax status of a partnership and the legal characteristics of a corporation, such as limited liability.

LLCs offer many advantages over other pass-through type entities, like partnerships and S corporations, such as the number and nature of its members, the ability to participate in the management of the business, and the way profits and losses can be allocated. In some cases a LLC could end up being taxed as a corporation so it is a good idea to consult with a CPA before making any final decision on a LLC.

Although LLCs appear favorable on the surface there are many traps for the unwary. To name a few, not all states recognize LLC status, distributions must be made in accordance with an operating agreement, and the conversion of an existing corporation to a LLC may trigger federal and state income taxes.

LLCs are ideal for family, start-up, and entrepreneurial businesses. LLCs are taxed the same way as a partnership. They use the same forms, 1065 and CT-1065, and the income is taxed at the individual level, not the entity level.

figure 9-2

Income Tax Checklist for a Partnership		
Type of Tax	Form Required	Due Date
Federal Taxes:		
Income Tax	Partner reports share of partnership income on Form 1040.	Same as Form 1040. (April 15th for calendar year individuals)
Self-Employment Tax	Partner reports share of partnership income subject to self employment tax on Schedule SE (Form 1040).	Same as Form 1040.
Estimated Tax	Partner includes partnership income, in calculating estimated tax payment requirement on 1040-ES.	15th day of 4th, 6th, and 9th months of tax year, and 15th day of 1st month after the end of tax year. (March 15, June 15, September 15 and January 15 for calendar year partnerships.)
Annual Return of Income	Partnership files Form 1065.	15th day of the 4th month after end of tax year. (April 15 for calendar year partnerships.)
State Taxes:		
Income Tax	Partner reports share of partnership income on Form CT-1040.	Same as federal.
Self Employment Tax	Not applicable.	Not applicable.
Estimated Tax	Partner includes partnership income in calculating estimated tax payment requirement on CT-1040ES.	Same as federal.
Annual Return of Income	Partnership files Form CT-1065.	Same as federal.

"C" CORPORATIONS

Net Income Taxed at Corporate Level

The net income of a "C" corporation is taxed at the corporate level. This is because a corporation is considered a separate entity for federal income tax purposes. A Corporation files a federal income tax return annually on either Form 1120, U.S. Corporation Income Tax Return, or Form 1120-A, U.S. Corporation Short Form Income Tax Return. It can get a six-month extension (Form 7004) for filing the return but not for paying the tax.

Like a sole proprietorship or partnership, a corporation's net income equals its gross income less allowable deductions. However, corporations are entitled to special deductions that other forms of business do not receive. These include a deduction for dividends received from other corporations and deductions for the owners' medical insurance and pension contribution.

Figure 9-3, on Page 9-10, is a summary of the "C" corporation's tax obligations. A complete checklist for the "C" corporation appears in Appendix G.

Assets of a Corporation

If a shareholder contributes assets to a corporation, the transaction usually doesn't create a tax gain or loss to the shareholder or the corporation. Once assets have been contributed to a corporation they are considered corporate assets for federal income tax purposes.

If a shareholder contributes property other than cash to a corporation, the corporation values the property at the shareholder's basis, regardless of the property's market value. The corporation then uses that basis for figuring depreciation and capital gains.

Withdrawals from Corporations - Double Tax

If a corporation pays a dividend, either in cash or property, the shareholder pays tax on the dividend. However, the dividend is not tax deductible for the corporation. Thus, both the corporation and the shareholder pay tax on the same income.

Not all distributions from corporations are taxable dividends. A corporation can make a *return of capital* distribution to shareholders. This occurs when the corporation has distributed all of its accumulated earnings and then makes another distribution. That distribution is considered a return of the shareholders' original capital in the corporation. A return of capital is not taxable. Distributions of property, returns of capital and complete liquidation of a corporation can pose federal income tax problems. In these complex situations the advice of a tax adviser is needed.

Status as Shareholder/Employee

Because a corporation is considered a separate taxable entity, a shareholder who works in the corporation is considered an employee, and cannot take *draws* as can a proprietor or partner. The company has to withhold taxes from the shareholder/employee's wages.

State Income Taxes

Unlike sole proprietorships or partnerships, Connecticut taxes a corporation as a separate entity. A profitable company's tax is figured on its net income, but there are three possible taxes: *income tax*, *capital tax* or *minimum tax*. The Connecticut corporation figures the tax all three ways and pays the highest one of the three.

Tax on Net Income

The starting point for determining state taxable income is federal taxable income. Specific adjustments are then made to either increase or decrease federal taxable income. Once federal taxable income has been determined the following additions and deductions are made to arrive at state taxable income:

> Additions include:
>> Interest income exempt from federal tax.
>> State income taxes.

> Deductions include:
>> Dividends received from other corporations.
>> Capital loss carryovers.
>> Operating loss carryovers.

The tax on net income is figured at a flat tax rate. There are two adjustments to this tax. One applies to corporations that do business in other states. Their tax is adjusted for profits that are taxed by other states. See *Doing Business in More Than One State* for more information. Another adjustment is for tax incentive credits, such as those for job development and neighborhood improvement.

See *State Tax Incentives* for more information. See Appendix R for the current Connecticut corporation tax rate.

Tax on Capital

The tax on capital is a tax on the average equity of the corporation. The tax is computed by multiplying the average equity by a flat tax rate. The tax rate is quite low, so the tax applies mainly to large corporations.

Minimum Tax

Connecticut charges a minimum tax of $250 even if the corporation has no taxable income.

A corporation computes its state tax on Form CT-1120. It can get a six-month extension for filing the return but not for paying the tax. It must pay the tax in four installments, discussed under *Estimated Taxes*, below.

figure 9-3

Income Tax Checklist for a "C" Corporation		
Type of Tax **Federal Taxes:**	Form Required	Due Date
Income Tax	Form 1120 or 1120A	15th day of 3rd month after end of tax year.
Estimated Tax	1120W (Deposits made with commercial bank)	15th day of 4th, 6th, 9th and 12th months of tax year.
State Taxes:		
Income Tax	Form CT-1120	First day of the 4th month after end of tax year.
Estimated Tax	Forms CT-1120 ESA, ESB, ESC, ESD.	15th day of 3rd, 6th, 9th and 12th months of tax year.

"S" CORPORATIONS

Requirements of an S Corporation

An "S" corporation is a corporation that elects to be exempt from federal income taxes. It is formed the same way as a "C" corporation and has the same legal protection and legal requirements as a "C" corporation. A corporation qualifies to be an "S" corporation by meeting five requirements. It must:

■ Be a corporation organized in the United States.

■ Have only one class of stock.

■ Have no more than 35 shareholders.

■ Have only individuals, estates and certain trusts as shareholders.

■ Have shareholders who are citizens or residents of the US.

Net income taxed at shareholder level

An "S" corporation is generally not a taxable entity. It files a separate U.S. Income Tax Return for an "S" corporation (Form 1120S), but it pays no tax to the IRS. Instead, the shareholders pay tax on their "S" corporation's taxable income on their personal tax returns. The shareholder receives a Schedule K-1 that lists the taxable share of "S" corporation income. This income is taxable even if the shareholder doesn't receive it. A shareholder's share of "S" corporation income is figured on ownership percentage. If there is an ownership change, the percentage is adjusted.

A summary of income tax requirements for an "S" corporation is found in Figure 9-4, on Page 9-13. A complete checklist of all taxes is found in Appendix F.

Assets of an "S" Corporation

If a shareholder contributes assets to an "S" corporation, the transaction usually doesn't create a tax gain or loss to the shareholder or the corporation. Once assets have been contributed to a corporation they are considered corporate assets for federal income tax purposes.

If a shareholder contributes property other than cash to an "S" corporation, the corporation values the property at the shareholder's basis, regardless of the property's market value. The corporation then uses that basis for figuring depreciation and capital gains.

Shareholder's basis in an "S" Corporation

Basis rules, similar to those for partnerships, apply to "S" corporations. These rules play a significant role in determining whether a shareholder can deduct "S" corporation losses. They are also instrumental in determining whether distributions from an "S" corporation are taxable or tax free. The rules for a partner's basis, on Page 9-5, are generally applicable to "S" corporations. However, only amounts loaned to the "S" corporation by the shareholder, rather than the share of the "S" corporations liabilities, operates to increase the shareholder's basis.

Withdrawals from "S" Corporations

The main benefit to organizing as an "S" corporation is the elimination of the double tax that applies to regular corporations. An "S" corporation's shareholder is taxed on income earned by the "S" corporation. Therefore, when an "S" corporation makes a dividend distribution to its shareholders, this distribution is generally tax free.

State income taxes

Connecticut "S" Corporations do not receive the special treatment they are allowed under federal tax law. Connecticut taxes them the same way as "C" Corporations. The exceptions are such items as interest income, dividends, rental income, capital gains and charitable contributions; these are passed directly to the "S" corporation shareholders, who report them on their personal income tax returns.

An "S" corporation uses Form CT-1120S to compute its state tax liability. Otherwise, the same adjustments, tax rates, estimated tax payment requirements, compliance procedures and other rules for "C" corporations apply to "S" corporations. A full explanation can be found in the "C" Corporation section starting on Page 9-8.

It is important to remember that Connecticut does not tax "S" corporation income at the individual level.

figure 9-4

Income Tax Checklist for an "S" Corporation		
Type of Tax **Federal Taxes:**	Form Required	Due Date
Income Tax	Form 1120S	15th day of 3rd month after end of tax year.
Estimated Tax	Shareholder includes "S" corporation income in calculating estimated tax payment requirements on 1040-ES	15th day of 4th, 6th, and 9th months of tax year, and 15th day of 1st month after the end of tax year.
State Income Taxes		
Income Tax	Form CT-1120S	First day of 4th month after end of tax year.
Estimated Tax	Form CT-1120S	15th day of 3rd, 6th, 9th, and 12th months of tax year.

CALCULATING NET INCOME

Gross income

The first step in calculating a company's net income is to compute gross income. Gross income includes any income received in the operation of a trade or business, such as income from the sale of products or services. It also includes interest, dividends or rents that the company receives. Gross income can be received in cash, property, or services.

Allowable deductions

From the gross income, the company deducts the expenses that are allowed in the tax code. This does not include *all* the company's expenses, because some are disallowed, and some are only partly deductible.

General rules of deductibility

To be deductible, a business expense must be ordinary in the business and necessary for its operation. An ordinary expense is one that is common and accepted in the line of business. A necessary expense is one that is helpful and appropriate for the business. All the expenses to be discussed in this section must first meet this test in order to be deductible. If an expense is partly for business and partly personal, the personal part must be separated from the business part, and only the business part is deductible.

Meal and entertainment expenses

Generally, in order to deduct meals and entertainment expenses, the company must be able to show that these expenses are:

■ Directly related to the active conduct of the business; or

■ Associated with the active conduct of the business. In this case, the meal or entertainment must directly precede or follow a substantial business discussion.

Meal and entertainment expenses falling into one of the two categories discussed above are generally only 50 percent deductible. The 50 percent limit applies to meal or entertainment expenses incurred while:

■ Traveling away from home (whether eating alone or with others) on business;

■ Entertaining business customers at your place of business, a restaurant, or other location; or

■ Attending a business convention or reception, business meeting, or business luncheon at a club.

Automobile expenses

The IRS rules for deducting expenses for business use of a car are very strict. Only business travel, not commuting to work, is allowed, and a car must be used more than 50% for business in order for expenses other than mileage to be deductible. *If* the car is used more than 50% for business, the owner is entitled to deduct reasonable operating costs, such as gas, garage rent, repairs, oil, licenses, tolls, lease fees, insurance, tires, parking fees, depreciation, car washes, property taxes, etc.

If a car is used for both business and personal purposes, the expenses are split between business and personal use. This may be done by keeping a log of business and personal mileage, and figuring a percentage split.

> *EXAMPLE*:
>
> A machine repairer drives a car 30,000 miles during the year, 20,000 miles for business and 10,000 miles for personal use. The repairer can claim only 67% (20,000 ÷ 30,000) of the car's operating cost as a business expense.

An alternative to figuring actual expenses is the standard mileage rate. The current standard mileage rate appears in Appendix R. To use the standard mileage rate, the taxpayer must:

- Own the car;
- Not use the car for hire (i.e., as a taxi); or
- Not operate a fleet of cars using two or more at the same time.

The standard mileage rate may only be chosen the first year the car is used for business. If the standard mileage rate isn't chosen in that first year, it can never be used for that car in any other year.

Interest expense

Interest expense for business is generally fully deductible, but the company must be able to prove that the money from the loan was used for a business purpose. If a business purpose can't be proved, the interest expense is classified as personal interest and isn't deductible.

Home office deductions

A home-based business can deduct some of the home expenses up to the limit of the gross income of the business. IRS rules for deducting a home office are very strict, and the owner should consult a tax adviser about them before taking the deduction. To be entitled to a home office deduction, the owner must use the office *exclusively* and *regularly*:

■ As the principal place of business;

■ As a place to meet or deal with patients, clients or customers in the normal course of business; or

■ In connection with the business if it is a separate structure that is not attached to the house.

Exclusive use means only for business. If the business office is also used for personal purposes, it does not meet the exclusive use test.

Regular use means on a continuing basis. Occasional or incidental business use does not meet the regular use test even if the office is not used for personal purposes.

The expenses are either fully or partly deductible. If the company is losing money, some of the expenses are carried over until there is a profit.

Fully Deductible	Expenses directly related to the business use of the home. These expenses include painting and repairs of areas used specifically for business.
Partly deductible	Expenses indirectly related to the business use of the home. These expenses include depreciation, utilities, repairs and maintenance, real estate taxes, insurance, rent, etc. To determine the amount of these expenses which are deductible as business expenses, multiply the total expense by the business percentage. The business percentage equals the area of the home used for business divided by the total area of the home. This area is expressed in square feet (SF). Thus, if the company's office has 100SF, the company's storage room is 50SF and the total house size is 2,000SF, the company can deduct 7½% of the house expenses $(100+50 \div 2000)$.

Travel expenses

Deductible travel expenses are ordinary and necessary expenses for travel away from home on business. This category does not include expenses that are for personal or vacation purposes. Examples of travel expenses include: airfare, meals and lodging, telephone expenses, etc. The fare paid for airplanes, trains, buses, taxis or other types of transportation is deductible. If the business trip is overnight or long enough to require rest, the cost of lodging is deductible. The actual cost of meals is generally deductible. However, a standard amount while traveling can be used. If the standard meal allowance is used, either $26 a day or $34 a day for certain locations in the United States is deductible. Although the standard meal allowance relieves the burden of keeping records of actual meal expenses, records still must be kept to prove the time, place, and business purpose of the travel. The current allowance rate can be found in Appendix R.

Equipment purchases and depreciation

Normally, equipment (or furniture, buildings, vehicles and similar assets that have useful lives of more than one year) can't be deducted as an expense in the year it is bought. There are two ways that these assets get deducted: depreciation and expensing.

Depreciation   This is a way of deducting the cost over several years. Each year, the company deducts the part of the original cost that *wears out* that year, based on the asset's useful life. The useful life is defined by IRS regulations. For example, if a machine costs $8,000 and has an 8-year useful life, the company can deduct $1,000 per year. The company also can use depreciation methods, described in IRS publication 534, that produce even larger deductions.

Expensing   A company also can deduct the full cost of a limited amount of new assets every year. This expensing deduction is currently limited to $17,500 per year and does not apply to real estate. Thus, a company could pay $4,000 for a computer setup and deduct it right away. If the company loses money, there is a further limitation to this deduction; it must be carried over until the company shows a profit.

Employee expenses

Salaries, wages, and other forms of pay to employees are deductible business expenses. There are four tests to determine whether payments to employees are deductible. The employees pay must be:

- Ordinary and necessary.
- Reasonable.
- For services performed.
- Paid or incurred.

Medical benefits

Insurance premiums paid to provide employees group medical benefits are generally fully deductible, and employees don't have to pay tax on the benefits they receive. Employee group plans, however, must provide continuation coverage to employees and their beneficiaries if they quit, get fired, laid off, become disabled or die.

Sole proprietors, partners and employees who own more than 2% of "S" corporations can only deduct 25% of their medical benefits cost. They do this on their personal tax returns. The owners of "C" corporations can deduct 100% of their medical benefits costs from the corporate profits.

Retirement benefits

Contributions to qualified retirement plans are generally deductible and employees aren't taxed on the contributions. They don't pay tax on the benefits until they receive them.

A qualified retirement plan must meet many strict requirements. These requirements include equitable coverage of employees, employees' entitlement to the money in their pension accounts and proper computing of contributions and benefits.

There are several different kinds of retirement plan, so a company owner should take the time to pick the right one. All companies can have either pension or profit-sharing plans. Proprietors and partners can have Keogh or HR-10 plans, designed for self-employed people and their employees. Small companies can have simplified employee pension (SEP) plans, which have very few administrative requirements. The company's CPA firm, brokerage firm or a pension consultant will help arrange a retirement plan.

Self-employment tax

Sole proprietors and partners do not have to pay social security tax; the self-employment tax is the proprietor's form of Social Security tax. Thus, the rate is linked to the Social Security tax rate. If they earn more than $400 being self-employed, they have to pay the self-employment tax in addition to regular taxes. The tax is figured on Schedule SE (Form 1040), Computation of Social Security Self-Employment Tax. Beginning in 1990, half of the self-employment income tax is deductible on the personal income tax form.

Expenses of starting a business

The costs to get ready to do business are not immediately deductible. Instead, these costs are deducted over a period of time, in the same way that equipment is depreciated. They are deducted as expenses in equal amounts over 60 months from the start-up of operations. If the business doesn't get started-up or if it fails, these expenses are deductible as a capital loss.

Nondeductible expenses - penalties/fines

Penalties or fines paid to the government for a violation of any law are not deductible. However, penalties paid for nonperformance of a contract or for late performance are generally deductible.

TAX COMPUTATION, CREDITS AND OTHER TAXES

Tax computation - general

The next step after calculating business gross income and allowable deductions, is to figure the net income or net loss. The step after that, figuring the tax, depends on the type of business organization.

For sole proprietorships, partnerships, LLCs or "S" corporations, the net income or loss is included in computing personal gross income. For "C" corporation, the corporation pays federal income taxes on its net income.

If an individual or a "C" corporation incurs a net loss, the loss can be carried back to offset net income in the three preceding years, resulting in a refund of prior year taxes paid. If any net loss remains after the carryback, the net loss can be carried forward to offset future net income for the next 15 years.

Tax incentives

Some business expenditures can produce tax credits. A tax credit is a direct reduction of tax liability. Two of the more common tax credits for small business owners are the jobs credit and the research credit.

Jobs Credit   The jobs credit is a percentage of wages paid to employees who are certified as members of a targeted group. Job credit wages are limited to $6,000 for each employee and $3,000 for each qualified summer youth employee.

Research Credit   The research credit is a percentage of expenses for research and experimental activities. The credit is 20 percent of the amount by which research expenses for the year exceed the average of a base period amount.

Proprietors, partners, LLCs and "S" corporation owners use the tax credits to offset federal income taxes on their personal income tax returns. A "C" corporation uses the tax credits on its federal income tax return.

State tax incentives

Connecticut also grants tax credits, but just to "C" and "S" corporations. These credits are direct reductions of the state tax liability. Listed below are some of the credit programs.

Neighborhood Assistance Program	This program allows a state tax credit of up to 60% of donations to approved child day care programs, employment and training programs, and programs for low-income people.
Contributions to Low and Moderate Income Housing Projects	A 100% credit is granted to corporations that donate to certain approved housing programs.
Manufacturing Facilities in Distressed Municipalities and Enterprise Zones	This credit is equal to 25% (50% for a qualifying facility in an enterprise zone) of the Connecticut tax allocable to certain approved manufacturing facilities.
Work Education	This credit is 10% of wages paid to a public high school student enrolled in an cooperative work education program.
Research and Development credit	A tax credit is allowed based on a specified percentage (ranging from 1% to 10%) of research and development expenses spent for R & D performed in Connecticut.
Machines and Equipment credit	A 5% or 10% credit (depending on size of corporation) is allowed for amounts spent for machines and equipment. (Effective 1/1/95)

Some other programs for which tax credits are granted are expenditures for air pollution abatement or industrial waste facilities, wages incurred for apprenticeships in machine tool and metal trades, expenditures for day care facilities and expenses for employee training.

OTHER TAX CONSIDERATIONS

Hobby loss rule

A tax pitfall to sole proprietors is the "hobby loss" rule, which disallows losses from activities that are hobbies rather than profit-making endeavors. The tax law presumes in general, that if an activity makes a profit for three years out of five, it is not a hobby. There are two exceptions.

One exception is for taxpayers who lose money in the first few years of operations. They can elect to postpone the three-year test until after their fifth year in business, by filing IRS Form 5213. This election operates as an *all or nothing* requirement. If the taxpayer passes the three-year test, all five years losses are deductible. Otherwise, none of them are.

Another exception is made for a taxpayers who can, despite having losses, prove the business was not a hobby. Factors that enter into this proof include the time and effort devoted to the business, the way the business is conducted, the expertise of the taxpayer, and the nature of the activity. However, it is up to the taxpayer to prove the profit motive behind the activity.

Alternative minimum tax

This tax was designed to ensure that businesses that receive special exemptions, deductions and credits wind up paying some minimum amount of tax. The alternative minimum tax applies in some way to all businesses. Proprietors, partners and "S" corporation owners pay it on their personal income tax returns. "C" corporations pay it directly.

In effect, the alternative minimum tax takes back special benefits that business owners receive. Every company should calculate its taxable amount before filing its tax return. In their tax planning, company managers should remember that the alternative minimum tax may cancel the benefits of jobs credit programs and other special tax benefits.

Doing business in more than one state

If a corporation does business only in Connecticut, all of its profit is taxed in Connecticut. But, if it is also doing business in other states, its profits may be taxable in those other states. Multi-state corporations must *apportion* their income among the states in which they operate. The general formula for this is found in the state tax returns and considers the locations of sales, employees wages and corporation property.

If a corporation sells in other states or has employees or property located outside Connecticut, it may have to pay income taxes to other states and should contact a tax advisor to check on state tax filing requirements.

Interest and penalties

Both the IRS and Connecticut charge penalties and interest to companies that do not follow the tax regulations. Among the many reasons that auditors can charge penalties are:

- Underpaying taxes.
- Late tax returns.
- Poor records.
- Failing to file returns.
- Substantially understating income tax liability.
- Negligence.

IRS penalties can go up to 25% of the tax due. Connecticut penalties are generally 10% of the tax due. The interest rate for late payment of IRS taxes is usually one or two percentage points over the Prime Rate. The rate for Connecticut is much higher: 1¼% per month or 15% per year.

The combined penalties and interest can easily double the tax of taxpayers who are careless about their tax obligations.

Audits

A tax audit can be conducted by mail or by personal interview. The IRS or the Connecticut Department of Revenue services decides on the method and notifies the taxpayer what records to provide.

A taxpayer can send someone else, such as a CPA or attorney, as a representative at the audit. The representative needs a written power of attorney to be able to speak for the taxpayer. Federal and state auditors use different power of attorney forms. For small companies, it is common for a representative to handle audits because of the potential for both additional taxes and penalties.

Statute of limitations

The statute of limitation defines the period in which the IRS and Connecticut may assess tax and the taxpayer may request a refund. Generally, the period is three years from the return's final due date or filing date or two years from the date the tax was paid. If a return is never filed or is filed fraudulently, the period remains open indefinitely. Both the IRS and Connecticut have administrative appeal procedures in case of a disagreement.

Information returns

Many small companies fail to file information returns and thereby expose themselves to penalties. The IRS form for these information returns is form 1099-MISC. It has to be given to payees during January every year. The table below lists the type of payment that must be reported and the limit for each type. If the limit is zero, all payments must be reported.

Rents	$600
Royalties	10
Prizes and Awards	600
Federal Income Tax Withheld	0
Fishing Boat Proceeds	0
Medical and Health Care Payments	600
Nonemployee Compensation	600
Dividends or Interest	10

The most commonly omitted 1099 form for small companies is the one for nonemployee compensation. This applies to subcontractors, consultants, CPAs, lawyers and other unincorporated payees who receive $600 or more. The penalty for failing to file a 1099 form is $50 per form.

ESTIMATED TAXES

Federal estimates

Federal payments depend on the type of business. Sole Proprietors, partners and "S" corporation owners have to make estimated tax payments if the total of their income tax and self-employment tax exceeds their total withholding and credits by $500 or more. These are paid with IRS Form 1040-ES, Estimated Tax for Individuals. Calendar year taxpayers make their estimated tax payments four times a year as follows:

Installment	Due Date
1	April 15th
2	June 15th
3	September 15th
4	January 15th (following year)

"C" corporations also make estimated tax payments if the tax for the year is expected to be $500 or more. These tax payments must be deposited at a bank, which transmits them to the IRS. They are due on the 15th day of the fourth, sixth, ninth and twelfth months of the corporation's fiscal year. For a calendar year corporation, they are as follows:

Installment	Due Date
1	April 15th
2	June 15th
3	September 15th
4	December 15th

There are underpayment penalties if the required estimated tax payments are not made by the due date. However, there are exceptions to reduce or eliminate the underpayment penalty. These are found in IRS Publication 334.

State estimates

Like Federal estimates, Connecticut estimate payments depend on the type of business: sole proprietorship, partnership, or corporation. The requirements are similar to those for the IRS, but more strict.

Sole Proprietors and Partners

These estimated tax payments are made at the individual level. Estimated tax payments are due four times a year:

Installment	Due Date
1	April 15th
2	June 15th
3	September 15th
4	January 15th (following year)

Corporations

Both "C" and "S" corporation have to make estimated tax payments to the state. If a corporation's tax liability is expected to exceed $1,000 or if the previous year's tax liability exceeded $1,000, it must make four estimated tax payments throughout the year. They are due on the 15th day of the third, sixth, ninth and twelfth months of the fiscal year. For a calendar year corporation, they are:

Installment	Due Date
1	March 15th
2	June 15th
3	September 15th
4	December 15th

"S" Corporation shareholders may also have to pay tax estimates for *pass through* items, such as interest, dividends, or rental income.

Connecticut, like the IRS, charges penalties for underpaying the estimated tax. Unlike the IRS, Connecticut offers very few exceptions to the rules for payment.

CONCLUSION

All company owners have to pay income taxes on the profits they earn. The way the company is taxed depends on which of the five organization structures was selected.

Most normal business expenses can be written off on the company's tax return, reducing the amount of tax paid. Some, however, are only partially deductible and some, like equipment, must be written off over several years.

Chapter 10
Sales, Excise and Property Taxes

INTRODUCTION

Besides income taxes, small businesses pay many other taxes. The income tax gets more publicity than other business taxes, but the other taxes could cost more. One of the most costly, payroll taxes, was discussed in Chapter 8, Payroll and Payroll Taxes. This chapter covers the others: Sales and Use, Excise, and Property.

The sales tax has long been the mainstay of Connecticut's revenue picture and will remain so for many years. Yet, it is widely misunderstood by owners of small companies. Many of these owners do not learn that their sales are taxable until an auditor comes to call.

This chapter discusses the sales tax and what things generally are taxable. It also tells how to find out if something is taxable, and discusses the audit and enforcement process.

ORGANIZATION OF CHAPTER

Connecticut sales and use tax
State and federal excise taxes
Property taxes

CONNECTICUT SALES AND USE TAX

The sales tax is the first tax a small business encounters. This tax covers equipment and services that are needed in order to start in business. It also covers services and products a business sells. Some business transactions are exempt from sales tax. It is important before starting the business to know what tax benefits the state allows and what the tax responsibilities are.

Of all of Connecticut's taxes, the sales and use tax is one of the largest revenue generators for the state. As one of the largest, the state aggressively seeks to assure that businesses are properly meeting their sales and use tax obligations. They do this by imposing high rates of interest and stiff penalties for not complying with the rules. Therefore, it is important to understand this tax well.

What follows is only a brief explanation of the sales and use tax. However, it should provide adequate knowledge and guidance to steer the new business owner in the right direction. First, we will look at who and what is subject to the tax. We will then look at a number of the exemptions allowed by the state. Finally, the material covers reporting procedures, forms and the state's audit procedures.

Who is subject to the tax

All businesses, regardless of legal form, are required to collect Connecticut sales tax from their customers on all taxable sales.

The sales tax is imposed for the privilege of making sales within Connecticut. The sales tax, although imposed on the business, is paid to the retailer by the consumer. It is the consumer who is liable to the retailer for the tax. The retailer in turn is liable to the state. Therefore, the retailer is acting as an agent of the state when collecting the sales tax from its customers.

What is taxable

The sales tax is imposed on retail sales of tangible personal property, the sale of a wide range of services and the leasing or rental of tangible personal property. It also is charged on hotel, inn and motel room rentals for less then 30 consecutive days.

Taxable Property

Only the sale or leasing of tangible personal property is subject to taxation. Therefore, the sale or leasing of buildings or land is not subject to the sales tax. However, not all tangible personal property is subject to tax. There are many exemptions, discussed later under *exempt property transactions*.

Taxable Services

Connecticut charges sales tax on many services. The list on the next page shows examples of twenty-one common taxable services.

Examples of taxable services

1. Computer and data processing services.
2. Painting and lettering services.
3. Private investigation and protection services.
4. Services to industrial, commercial or income producing real property.
5. Business analysis, management consulting and public relations services.
6. Motor vehicle repair services.
7. Certain agent relationship services.
8. Locksmith services.
9. Landscaping and horticulture services.
10. Maintenance and janitorial services.
11. Exterminating services.
12. Swimming pool cleaning and maintenance services.
13. Repair or maintenance service including any contract of warranty or service.
14. Miscellaneous personal services such as photographic studio services.
15. Renovation services such as paving, painting, wallpapering, roofing, siding.
16. Advertising or public relation services.
17. Tax preparation services.
18. Transportation services.
19. Room occupancy in hotels and lodging houses.
20. Health and athletic club services.
21. Transportation charges on taxable sales.

This is not an exhaustive list of all the taxable services. There are hundreds of taxable services.

There are uncertainties in most categories of taxable services, and many disagreements between taxpayers and the state about interpretations of the law. Owners of service-oriented companies *must* consult with a tax advisor or call the Department of Revenue Services before starting-up to find out about sales taxes on their services.

Tax rate

The sales tax is based on a percentage of gross receipts from sales. A reduced rate is provided for repair or replacement parts that are exclusively for use on manufacturing machinery. The purchaser can claim a refund from the state, up to $7,500, for tax paid on these purchases. The current sales tax rate is listed in the tax table in Appendix R.

When and where is the sale taxable

When and where the Connecticut tax applies depends upon whether the sale is property or a service. The table below shows the difference.

Taxable Property   Tangible personal property is taxed at the time the transfer of title to the personal property occurs. Title must pass in Connecticut in order for the sale to be taxed in Connecticut.

Taxable Services   A service is taxed at the time it is performed. The tax on services generally occurs where the benefit of the service is realized and not necessarily where it is performed. The service must generally be received by the purchaser in Connecticut in order to be taxed in Connecticut.

Who and what is exempt from tax

Not all sales of tangible personal property and services are subject to the tax. There are numerous exceptions. It is beyond the scope of this chapter to cover all of the exceptions. Only the major exceptions will be covered to give a flavor of the depth and breadth of the exemptions. The list below gives two categories of exemption: exempt customers and exempt property.

Exempt Customer   Examples of customers who don't have to pay sales tax:

United States Government.
Connecticut Government.
Nonprofit charitable hospitals.
Charitable and religious organizations.
People making purchases with federal food stamps.
Certain service centers for the elderly.
Low and moderate income housing facilities.

Exempt Property   Some sales are not taxable at all regardless of who the customer is. Examples of exempt transactions:

Purchases for resale.
Sales exempt under United State laws.
Clothing costing less than $50.
Prescription medicine and medical equipment.
Food products except meals in restaurants.
Motor vehicles not registered in Connecticut.
Printed material for delivery outside Connecticut.
Fuel used for heating.
Component parts used to assemble manufacturing machinery.
Manufacturing machinery.
Printing machinery.
Replacement parts for machinery in enterprise zones.

Exemption Certificates

Of the exemptions listed above, three deserve further explanation: Resale Exemption, Machinery Exemption, and Charitable and Religious Organization Exemption. To get these exemptions, the purchaser must give the seller an exemption certificate. It is not enough for the seller to rely on the name of the purchaser, or the apparent destination of the sale. The seller must have the necessary certificate on file to prove the exemption. Otherwise, a tax auditor can demand that the seller pay the tax anyway.

There is a different certificate for each situation:

■   *Resale*: Resale Certificate.
■   *Machinery, Tools and Materials*: Manufacturing Exemption Certificate.
■   *Charitable and Religious Organizations*: Charitable/Religious Exemption Certificate.

Charitable and religious organizations are required to have special state exemption permits. The exemption certificate must contain the organization's exempt permit number.

The exemption certificate is an important bit of self-protection for the seller. In general, having one means that the purchaser will have to pay the sales tax if it is later determined that a sale was taxable. Purchasers do not have to file their certificates with the state. The seller *must* keep a copy of all exemption certificates to prove that sales were tax-free.

The only requirement is that the seller accept the exemption certificate in good faith. If so, the seller will generally be relieved of liability. Good faith is having a reasonable belief that a resale certificate is valid.

Employees versus independent contractors

If an employee performs a taxable service for an employer for a salary, the service isn't taxable. If an independent contractor does the same service for a fee, the service is taxable. For example, if a consultant does consulting as an independent contractor for a fee, the service is taxable. If the same person is hired as an employee for a salary, the service isn't taxable.

Use tax and out of state purchases

Connecticut's use tax is a widely misunderstood tax. A use tax is really a sales tax charged in two situations: out-of-state purchases and in-state purchases on which no sales tax was charged. The use tax rate is the same as the sales tax rate and the tax is paid with the same form as the sales tax.

Most small businesses encounter the use tax on out-of-state purchases. As a rule, if an out-of-state transaction would have been taxable in Connecticut, it is subject to use tax. For example, if a company buys something in Vermont for use in Connecticut, it must pay Connecticut use tax on the purchase. If the Vermont vendor charges Vermont sales tax, Connecticut allows a credit for the sales tax already paid. If the company makes a mail order purchase and the seller charges no sales tax, it must pay the full Connecticut sales tax on the purchase.

Even if the purchase takes place in Connecticut, there may still be a use tax on it. For example, if a company buys something for resale, which is exempt, but then uses the item in the business instead of reselling it, it has to pay a use tax.

Procedures and forms

Connecticut charges a high rate of interest and stiff penalties for not meeting sales tax obligations. The sales tax law dictates the time for paying taxes, the forms and the due dates.

When the Tax Is Due to the State

In general, the tax must be reported in the period when the property is sold or when the service is provided, not when it is paid for. Thus, if a company makes a sale in March and receives payment in April, the sales tax must be reported in the March quarter, not the June quarter. If the customer doesn't pay, or returns the merchandise, the state refunds the tax paid, or allows a credit on the next sales tax payment. The seller must be able to prove that the account was uncollectible.

The exception to this general rule is for service providers that use the cash basis of reporting on their income tax returns. They are allowed to pay the sales tax on the cash basis, when they get paid, rather than when they provide the service. Companies that use the accrual method for income taxes must still pay the tax when the service is provided.

Forms to File and Paying Tax

The same form, OS-114 applies to all sales and use tax payments. The return and payment are due on the last day of the month after the reporting period. For example, if the tax period ends in June, the tax must be paid by the end of July. This reporting period is either annually, quarterly or monthly:

- **Annual**: Taxpayers whose total tax liability for the 12-month period ending on the preceding September 30th was less than $1,000.

- **Quarterly**: New taxpayers or taxpayers whose total tax liability for the 12-month period ended on the preceding September 30th was less than $4,000.

- **Monthly**: All other taxpayers.

The table in Figure 10-1, on the next page, illustrates the payment rules.

figure 10-1

Example - Sales tax payment dates		
Threshold	Reporting Period	Due Date
Taxpayer whose annual tax liability is less than $1,000	January-December	January 31 of next year
New Taxpayer	January, February, March	April 30
Tax liability was less than $4,000 for the 12 months ending on the preceding September 30	January, February, March	April 30
Tax liability was $4,000 or more for the 12 months ending on the preceding September 30	January	February 28

An extension to file the return may be granted under certain circumstances, such as illness or personal hardship. However, this does not extend the time to pay the tax.

A return must be filed even if no tax is due or no sales were made during the reporting period.

Penalty and Interest

The penalty for failing to file a sales tax return or failing to pay the tax when it is due is generally 15% of the tax due. In addition, the state charges interest for late payments. The rate is 1⅔% per month (20% annually) from the due date of the return to the date of payment.

Audits

Connecticut generally has 3 years from the time the business files its tax return to perform an audit and assess additional taxes. If no return is filed the audit time period is unlimited; the state auditors can audit as far back as they want.

The audits are done by professional auditors from the Department of Revenue Services (DRS). If the taxpayer disagrees with the DRS auditor, the department has an administrative appeal procedure. If that fails, the taxpayer can still go to court to resolve the dispute.

In a typical audit, the auditor reviews more than one year. In most cases, the auditor will look at transactions for a period of three years.

The auditor will generally look at three areas: fixed asset purchases, recurring expenditures, and gross receipts. There are different approaches to each area:

Fixed Asset Purchases

Under the first category the auditor looks at the company's tangible personal property purchases during the audit period to determine if Connecticut sales or use tax was paid. The auditor normally wants to see the invoice for each fixed asset purchase. One focus is on out-of-state vendors to determine that the taxpayer paid a use tax to Connecticut. Another is on items that may have been purchased with a resale or manufacturing exemption certificate and used for something else.

Recurring Expenditures

These are the company's administrative or overhead expenses, such as office supplies, repairs, etc. The auditor normally does not look at all at expenditures for the whole audit period but instead selects a sample period, such as 1 to 6 months, and looks at expenditures during that period. Based on the error rate in this sample method, the auditor figures a tax for the entire period. For example, if the auditor finds that 5% of the expenditures in the sample period didn't get taxed properly, the company will be charged an extra tax on 5% of the expenditures during the entire audit period.

Gross Receipts

The third target area in an audit is the company's sales. The auditor first checks to see that the sales reported on the sales tax returns equals the sales reported on the company's Federal income tax return. If the income tax return's sales are more than those reported on sales tax returns, the auditor asks for an explanation for the difference. If the difference can't be explained, the company can be charged sales tax on the difference.

Next, the auditor looks at sales to see if the tax was figured correctly, collected and paid on time. Here, too, the auditor uses a sample approach and figures a tax assessment based on the findings for a small part of the company's sales. The emphasis is generally on exempt sales and out-of-state sales.

To prepare for a sales tax audit, or to prevent problems in case there is an audit, company personnel should follow a five step process:

1. Review all fixed asset invoices to be sure tax was paid.

2. Reconcile sales reported on the Federal income tax return with that shown on sales tax returns.

3. Review supplies and other recurring expenditure invoices for sales tax applicability.

4. Keep a three-ring binder or file folder of exemption certificates received. Be sure there is an exemption certificate to support every exempt sale. Don't take a customer's word that a sale is exempt. Either request a certificate or collect the sales tax.

5. When making an out-of-state purchase, if the purchase would be taxable in Connecticut, either ask the seller to collect the sales tax and remit it to the State of Connecticut or report the purchase and pay use tax on it.

STATE AND FEDERAL EXCISE TAXES

Connecticut charges excise taxes which are administered by state agencies. An excise tax is a special form of sales tax. Current tax rates are used for discussion purposes, but the rates are subject to change at any time. This includes taxes on:

Alcoholic beverages

Each distributor of alcoholic beverages must pay a tax on all sales of alcoholic beverages. Alcoholic beverages include spirits, wine, beer and liquor. The tax is generally imposed on a per barrel or per gallon basis. The tax ranges from $6.00 per barrel of beer and $4.50 per gallon of liquor, to 60 cents per gallon of still wines. The tax is paid monthly with the filing of a return to the state.

Cigarette and tobacco products

A stamp tax is imposed on all cigarettes held in-state for sale. The tax is paid by purchasing stamps from the state then sticking them on to the cigarette packages. The tax is on a per cigarette basis; the tax rate for a pack of 20 cigarettes is 47 cents. There are certain exemptions from the stamp tax such as previously taxed imported cigarettes. An excise tax is also imposed on tobacco products (other than cigarettes) such as cigars, smoking tobacco, and chewing tobacco. The tax is imposed at the rate of 20% of the wholesale sales price. The tax is paid monthly with the filing of a return to the state.

Cabaret admissions and club dues

A 10% tax applies to all the admission charges to any place of amusement, entertainment or recreation and a 5% tax applies to amounts charged for refreshments, service or merchandise at places furnishing public performances (such as cabarets). There are exemptions from the tax, such as admissions to nonprofit playhouses.

Motor fuels, gasoline and special fuels

Distributors must pay a tax on each gallon of fuel sold. Fuel includes gasoline, gasohol, and diesel. The rate of tax depends on the type of fuel sold: gasoline -

30 cents per gallon, gasohol - 29 cents per gallon, diesel - 18 cents per gallon. Certain sales of fuel are exempt from tax. For example, fuel sold which will be used exclusively for heating purposes is exempt from the tax. The tax is paid monthly with the filing of a return to the state.

Motor carrier

A motor carrier road tax applies to certain motor carriers operating on Connecticut highways. The tax is based on the amount of fuel used by a motor carrier in its operation in the state and the tax rate is the same as the motor fuels rate. The tax is paid quarterly with the filing of a return to the state.

Petroleum

A tax is imposed on the distribution of petroleum products in the state. The tax only applies to the first in-state use of the petroleum product. The tax is based on the quarterly gross earnings. The tax rate is 5% and is paid quarterly with the filing of a return to the state.

The federal government also charges excise taxes on certain business activities. Federal excise taxes are organized into seven major groups:

1. Environmental.
2. Communication and air transportation.
3. Fuel.
4. Luxury.
5. Retail and use.
6. Manufacturing.
7. Other miscellaneous.

Within each of these major groups there are several specific excise taxes.

If the company is doing business in any of these areas, it may have to pay excise tax. Contact a tax advisor, the Internal Revenue Service or the DRS to get more information. Publication 510, obtained from the IRS, discusses specific details about federal excise taxes. It also explains IRS Form 720, the Quarterly Federal Excise Tax Return.

PROPERTY TAXES

Depending on the type of business, property taxes may be a large tax liability. It is important to have a basic understanding of how Connecticut taxes property owners.

Taxable property

There are no state property taxes. Instead, property taxes are assessed by local governments. In Connecticut, the town or city is the taxing unit for assessing and collecting property taxes. In general, all real estate and personal property in Connecticut is taxable unless it is specifically exempt from tax. There are many exemptions and it is not practical to explain all of them in detail here. The next section is a general explanation of the exemptions.

Exemptions

Exemptions generally include inventories of manufacturers and mercantile operations, acquisitions of new manufacturing machinery and equipment, computer software, and manufacturing facilities and equipment operating in an enterprise zone. The property owned by various organizations are also exempt, such as the property owned by nonprofit charitable, educational, religious and scientific organizations, as discussed in Chapter 11.

Rate of tax

Property is taxed at a uniform percentage, currently 70%, of the assessed value. For real estate, the town uses an appraisal to figure the assessment. For business equipment, the town uses the company's cost. The taxable basis of equipment is adjusted downward for older equipment. Appeals from assessments may be made to the town's board of tax review.

The tax rate is determined by the local tax district and as a result, varies from town to town. Rates vary from about $13 to $80 per $1,000 of assessed value.

Form to file

All business property owners have to file a return on or before November 1st of each year listing all taxable property they owned on the assessment date, October 1st. The towns charge interest if the tax isn't paid on time.

Audits

Many towns hire outside auditors to help them with taxpayer compliance. The town and the auditor first look for companies that aren't filing property tax returns. They do this by cross-checking Yellow Pages and newspaper advertising against their records, by checking business directories and similar techniques. Then, they visit the company to check the declared valuations against property on hand. They are allowed to look at the company books and tax returns in order to check on valuations. Property owners can appeal valuations.

CONCLUSION

At least annually, it's a good idea to review the company's sales, excise and property tax situation. The following is a checklist of things to look for:

- Review the possibility of sales and use tax exemptions for that of the business and that of customers.

- Invoices should be reviewed for sales and use tax applicability.

- Review the possibility of hiring an employee as opposed to an independent contractor.

- Consider Federal and state excise tax responsibilities.

- Review with municipality personnel the types of property that may be exempt from property taxes.

- If property has recently been revalued by municipality, review assessed value to ascertain its reasonableness in light of local conditions.

- Companies that are located in enterprise zones may be eligible for corporate tax credits, property tax abatement, exemption from sales and use taxes as well as a variety of other state and local incentives. Consult your town hall to see if your business is located in an enterprise zone.

Chapter 11
Not-For-Profit Organizations

INTRODUCTION

Not-for-profit organizations meet big challenges to house the homeless, provide caring environments for AIDS victims, nurture preschool children, or fulfill other worthwhile goals.

Organization leaders must develop active, efficient service organizations and complete many financial tasks in order to set up their organizations. These tasks include applying for federal tax exempt status, registering as not-for-profit enterprises in Connecticut, filing annual information returns, developing Boards of Directors and maintaining effective financial controls.

ORGANIZATION OF CHAPTER

Benefits of tax-exempt status
Eligibility for tax-exempt status
Starting a not-for-profit organization
Qualifying for tax-exempt status
Reports due by tax-exempt organizations

BENEFITS OF TAX-EXEMPT STATUS

Generally, the most attractive feature of becoming a not-for-profit organization is the ability to avoid taxes on funds received to meet the organization's tax-exempt purpose.

In addition to exemption from federal and state income tax, not-for-profit organizations may receive property tax and sales and use tax exemptions.
Payroll of a not-for-profit organization is exempt from Federal unemployment taxes if the organization is a 501(c)(3) organization as described below. This is the tax paid annually on Form 940. Not-for-profit organizations are also eligible to receive preferred postal rates. And, of course, contributions to public charities and not-for-profit organizations exempt under Internal Revenue Service Code

Section 501(c)(3) which are not classified as private foundations, are deductible on individual and corporate income tax returns, subject to certain limitations.

ELIGIBILITY FOR TAX-EXEMPT STATUS

The Internal Revenue Service grants tax-exempt status to two types of organizations:

■ Section 501(c)(3) organizations.

■ Other Section 501(c) organizations.

Section 501(c)(3) organizations

This category includes organizations that provide a service to the general public. It includes six groups of organizations:

1. Churches and church associations.

2. Educational organizations such as schools and colleges.

3. Hospitals and their medical research organizations.

4. Organizations operated for the benefit of state and municipal colleges and universities.

5. Government units.

6. Publicly supported organizations. These are organizations that receive at least one-third of their support from the general public or governments.

Some organizations do not receive one-third of their support from the general public or governmental units. These organizations can still be tax exempt if the facts support it and if they receive over 10% of their support from the public or government. They must also be organized and operated so as to attract continuous government and public support.

Other Section 501(c) organizations

Many other organizations can receive the benefits of tax-exempt status, other than the receipt of deductible charitable contributions. These organizations include, but are not limited to, employee associations, labor organizations, chambers of commerce and social clubs.

STARTING A NOT-FOR-PROFIT ORGANIZATION

The first step in starting a not-for-profit organization is to create an organization document. This document, known as a charter, constitution or articles of incorporation, is important for all types of business groups. But, it is especially important for not-for-profit organizations because the Internal Revenue Service uses it to test their eligibility for tax-exempt status. An organization document is usually prepared by an attorney. To pass Internal Revenue Service scrutiny, it must do these things:

■ **Mission** - Clearly and briefly define a mission. The mission is a statement of the actions the organization will take to accomplish its goals. Besides helping with IRS approval, a clear mission can also make it easier to move community members to action and to raise funds.

■ **Limits of Power** - Limit the purposes and powers of the organization to tax exempt purposes. It cannot allow the organization, except for a minor part of its activities, to do things that are not related to its exempt purposes.

■ **Use of funds** - Prohibit the organization's net earnings from being used to benefit private individuals.

■ **Legislation** - Prohibit the organization from influencing legislation or campaigning for or against candidates for public office. It can elect to come under provisions allowing limited lobbying expenditures.

■ **Dissolution** - Require that, if it goes out of business, the assets be distributed to another exempt organization or transferred to a federal, state or local government for a public purpose.

A helpful publication in determining tax-exempt status is Internal Revenue Service Publication 557, "Tax-Exempt Status for Your Organization." This publication is a detailed review of the many types and qualifications of tax-exempt organizations.

Once the organization document has been created, the organization must incorporate as a non-stock, nonprofit corporation by registering with the Connecticut Secretary of State and paying the necessary fees.

In order for an organization to become a not-for-profit organization, it must first qualify as one. Later, it must file special reports with the IRS, and sometimes with Connecticut. A summary of the application forms and reports appears in Figures 11-1, below and 11-2, on Page 11-5.

figure 11-1

Connecticut forms	
Form Number and Name	Explanation
Application forms:	
CPC-63 Registration Statement	Registration with Connecticut Department of Consumer Protection Public Charities Unit.
CPC-54 Exempt Verification Status	Verification of exempt status also filed with the Public Charities Unit.
Annual information return:	
CPC-60 Annual Report Face Sheet	Accompanied by IRS Form 990. If gross revenues exceed $100,000, a complete set of audited financial statements is sent to the State.

figure 11-2

IRS forms and publications

Form Number and Name	Explanation
Application Forms:	
1023, 1024 Tax Exemption Applications	Application for exemption from income tax. Necessary for eligibility for other nonprofit advantages.
SS-4 Application for Federal Employer Identification Number (FEIN)	Registers the organization with the IRS. FEIN is a prerequisite for issuing payroll and is used as the organization's identification number when corresponding with the IRS.
Annual Information Returns:	
990 and Schedule A Returns of Organization Exempt from Income Tax	Reports financial information including Statement of Revenue and Expenses and Balance Sheet for past fiscal year. Also requests information on such things as program activities, certain contributions to the organization and the names of board members. Schedule A requests supplemental information on the sources of financial support necessary to maintain tax-exempt public charity status.
990EZ	Shortened version of Form 990 for organizations with gross receipts less than $100,000 and end of year total assets of less than $250,000.
990-T Exempt Organization Business Income Tax Return	Filing of financial information if gross unrelated business income exceeds $1,000. Must be filed on or before the regular due date for Form 990.
2758 Application for Extension of Time to File	Extends deadline for Form 990, Schedule A and Form 990-T (if your organization is formed as a trust) for up to two months. Three (3) extensions may be requested. Extension maximum of six months.
7004 Application of Extension of Time to File	Extends deadline for tax-exempt corporations who must file a 990-T for six months.
Other IRS Forms:	
1128 Application for Change in Accounting Period	Must be submitted and approved by IRS before any changes in accounting period can be made.
5768 Election/Revocation of Election by an Eligible Section 501(c)(3) Organization	To elect to expend a limited but more than "insubstantial" amount of expenditures on lobbying.

QUALIFYING FOR TAX-EXEMPT STATUS

In order to qualify for tax-exempt status, an organization must file applications with both the federal government and Connecticut.

Federal Qualification

To be exempt from federal tax, an organization must file an application along with a $500 fee to the Internal Revenue Service. Depending on the type of organization, it files either Form 1023 or Form 1024.

Form 1023

Form 1023 is the initial application for exemption under **Section 501(c)(3)** of the Internal Revenue Code. This form should be filed within fifteen months from the end of the month in which the organization was formed. The organization will also have to include its Articles of Incorporation and its Bylaws, along with selected financial information and information about its founders. If tax-exempt status is granted, it is retroactive to the date the not-for-profit organization was formed.

Once the Internal Revenue Service receives Forms 1023, it issues a definitive or an advance ruling regarding the organization's status as a public charity or private foundation. Private foundations must meet more stringent standards than public charities; e.g. private foundations are required to distribute annual income and may possibly be required to pay excise taxes.

If an organization receives an advance ruling, it must submit information indicating that it has met the public support test during the five years of the advance ruling period. If this information does not indicate that the organization met the public support test, the organization will have to pay excise taxes as if it were a private foundation.

Form 1024

Form 1024 it the application for exemption under **Section 501(a)** or for Determination under Section 120. This form is used to obtain exempt status for other organizations such as civic leagues, social and recreational clubs, employees' associations.

Connecticut Qualification

To be exempt from Connecticut corporation tax, an organization must send a copy of the 501(c) ruling received from the Internal Revenue Service stating that the organization is exempt from federal tax. Connecticut will exempt the organization from the state corporation income tax and no annual tax return will be due to the state.

An organization that has been granted exemption from federal tax can get an exemption from sales tax on purchases in Connecticut by sending the following documents to the Legal Division of the Department of Revenue Services:

■   A copy of the 501(c)(3) ruling letter from the Internal Revenue Service.

■   A copy of the by-laws.

■   A copy of the latest financial statement.

■   A notarized statement from the President of the organization that the organization is not subject to property tax.

■   A cover letter requesting exemption from sales tax.

Small not-for-profit groups such as accredited schools, little leagues, scouts and parent teacher organizations are not required to register with the Department of Revenue Service to collect sales tax on items sold if the items are sold for $20 or less and the purpose is to raise funds for youth activities. Other organizations would have to collect sales tax on taxable items sold to raise funds.

The Connecticut Solicitation of Charitable Funds Act requires charitable organizations to register before they can solicit funds. An organization registers by filing Registration Form CPC-63 with the state's Public Charities Unit and paying a $20 registration fee. Registration is a one-time task; there is no annual renewal.

Some organizations are exempt from registration. There are six categories:

1. Religious corporations, institutions, or societies.

2. Parent-teacher organizations and educational institutions, if they have been properly registered.

3. Non-profit hospitals.

4. Government agencies.

5. Solicitors of funds for the above organizations.

6. Charitable organizations that do not pay anyone to solicit contributions, and receive under $25,000 annual contributions of money, credit, property, financial assistance, etc. The $25,000 limit does not include membership dues.

An organization that falls within one of these six categories must verify its exemption from registration by filing Form CPC-54, Exempt Status Verification. There is no filing fee and no other form need be filed in the future if the organization qualifies as exempt, although the Department of Consumer Protection can require continued proof of exemption.

REPORTS DUE BY TAX-EXEMPT ORGANIZATIONS

An organization may have to file annual informational returns with both the federal government and Connecticut depending on the type of organization, its annual gross receipts and its total assets at year end.

Federal Reports

Not-for-profit organizations may have to file Internal Revenue Service Form 990, Return of an Organization Exempt from Income Tax, or Form 990EZ, Short Form Return of Organization Exempt From Income Tax. An organization can use Form 990EZ instead of Form 990 if its gross receipts for the year were less than $100,000 and its total assets at the end of the year were less than $250,000. Certain types of organizations such as schools, religious organizations or state institutions are not required to file at all. Also, an organization whose annual gross receipts are normally less than $25,000 does not have to file.

If an organization is required to file Form 990 or 990EZ, it is due 5½ months after the end of the organization's tax year. Form 990 and 990EZ's Schedule A, includes information about activities of charitable organizations that claim "public charity" status.

Late filing or failing to file, without a good reason, can cost an organization a penalty of $10 per day up to a maximum of $5,000. Even incomplete filings can cost penalties. The Internal Revenue Service can reject an incomplete Form 990 or 990EZ charge the same penalty as if the form had never been filed.

The due dates of Forms 990 and 990EZ can be extended by filing Form 2758 with the Internal Revenue Service by the due date of the return. By filing successive Forms 2758 for three months each, the time for filing a Form 990 or 990EZ can be extended a maximum of six months.

Every organization with gross unrelated business income of $1,000 or more must file Form 990-T, Exempt Organization Business Income Tax Return, by the fifteenth day of the fifth month after the close of the not-for-profit organization's year. 'Unrelated trade or business' is any trade or business which is *not substantially related* to the organization's exempt purpose. This is discussed in detail in IRS Code Section 513(a). The due date of Form 990-T can be automatically extended six months by filing Form 7004.

Tax-exempt organizations must make a copy of its three most recent annual information returns available for public inspection. Failure to comply with this requirement of public inspection may result in a $10 per day (maximum of $5,000 per annual return) penalty.

Tax-exempt organizations must withhold and deposit payroll taxes for employees and file quarterly payroll tax returns. These are the federal income tax and the social security taxes withheld and reported on Form 941.

Connecticut Reports

An organization does not have to file a state form comparable to the Federal Form 990 with Connecticut. However, if it is registered with the state to solicit funds, it must file Form CPC-60, Annual Report Face Sheet and a copy of its Internal Revenue Service Form 990 or 990EZ within five months after the end of its tax year. If the organization collects more than $100,000 in gross revenue, not including government grants and fees, it has to have an audit by a Certified Public Accountant. The audit report can range from an accountant's report on the Internal Revenue Service Form 990 to a complete set of audited financial statements. There is a $25 filing fee for the CPC-60. The organization can get a three month filing extension from the Public Charities Unit by writing a letter to the unit.

Information about the Connecticut Solicitation of Charitable Funds Act and filing forms can be obtained from the state agency that oversees the law:

> Public Charities Unit
> Department of Consumer Protection
> c/o Office of the Attorney General
> 55 Elm Street
> Hartford, Connecticut 06106
> Telephone: (203) 566-5836

CONCLUSION

Tax-exempt organizations receive many benefits, such as exemption from federal tax, relief from Federal unemployment taxation and property and sales tax exemptions. Many organizations find it time-consuming to become tax-exempt, and the process does contain some traps for the unwary. The annual state and federal reporting requirements are very different from those for profit-making businesses.

This discussion was intended as an overview, not to cover all exempt organization issues. Organizations that seek tax-exempt status will find it worthwhile to use professional guidance.

ORDER FORM

for

STARTING A SMALL BUSINESS IN CONNECTICUT

Fill out and return to:

Community Accounting Aid & Services, Inc.
1800 Asylum Avenue, 4th Floor
West Hartford, CT
06117

Please send me a copy of the new Starting a Small Business in Connecticut. Enclosed is a check for $28.95 made payable to CAAS.

(The price equals $24.95 plus sales tax of $1.50 and shipping/handling of $2.50).

Name:_____

Address:_____

City:_____ State:_____ Zip:_____

Daytime Telephone:_____

If you would like to order more than one copy, please call the CAAS office at 241-4984 to obtain correct pricing.

- -

ORDER FORM

for

STARTING A SMALL BUSINESS IN CONNECTICUT

Fill out and return to:

Community Accounting Aid & Services, Inc.
1800 Asylum Avenue, 4th Floor
West Hartford, CT
06117

Please send me a copy of the new Starting a Small Business in Connecticut. Enclosed is a check for $28.95 made payable to CAAS.

(The price equals $24.95 plus sales tax of $1.50 and shipping/handling of $2.50).

Name:_____

Address:_____

City:_____ State:_____ Zip:_____

Daytime Telephone:_____

If you would like to order more than one copy, please call the CAAS office at 241-4984 to obtain correct pricing.

Appendix

Appendix A - Business start-up checklist

Item	Form Number
Organization - normally done by corporate attorney:	
Fictitious name (if any)	
Corporate name	61-1, 61-3
Certificate of incorporation	61-5
Registration with Secretary of State	61-6, 61-7A
Common stock/stock books	
Shareholders' or partners' agreement	
Corporate minute book and organization meeting minutes	
Business license (repairer, remodeler, etc.)	Various
Tax - normally done by CPA and company bookkeeper:	
State I.D. No./Sales tax no.	Reg-1
Federal I.D. No.	SS-4
State unemployment compensation registration	CT UC-1A
Withholding certificates-all employees	W-4
"S" corporation election (within 75 days of formation)	2553
Employment eligibility verification	I-9

Accounting - normally done by CPA and company personnel:
Chart of accounts (account categories for income and expenses)
Cash disbursements and payroll records and procedures
Cash receipts and receivables records and procedures
Inventory records and procedures
Monthly close-out procedures
Organization date balance sheet

Banking - normally done by company's lead bank:
Savings or money market account
Operating account

Insurance - normally done by company with insurance agent:
Business liability
Business casualty
Business interruption
Group medical, life and disability benefits
Workers' compensation
Product liability
Directors' liability
Vehicle liability/casualty

Appendix B - Business plan contents

Narrative section
    Introduction
    Business purpose
        Product or service
        Product positioning
        Company history
    Marketing
        Company location
        Demographics
        Market segment
        Competition
        Market data (summarized)
        Sales plans
        Advertising plans
        Promotion plans
    Organization
        Legal structure
        Management assignments
        Key personnel
        Training needs and plans
        Names and addresses of key business advisors
    Summary
        Summarized financial data
        Summarized market data

Financial section
    Projected balance sheet
    Projected income statement
    Projected statement of cash flow
    Assumptions used in preparing projections
    Start-up expense budget

Appendix
    Owners' résumés
    Top managers' résumés
    Market data
    Photographs of products
    Organization charts

Appendix C - Forms to file in order to start up in Connecticut

Form Name	Form	State/Fed	Proprietor	Partnership	LLC	S Corp	C Corp	Nonprofit
Application for Employer Number	SS-4	F	(1)	Y	Y	Y	Y	Y
Election by a Small Business Corporation	2553	F	N	N	N	Y	N	N
Application for Recognition of Exemption	1023	F	N	N	N	N	N	Y
Application for State Tax Registration Number	Reg 1	S	(1)	Y	Y	Y	Y	Y
Application for State Unemployment Number	UC-1A	S	(1)	Y	Y	Y	Y	(1)
Registration of Fictitious Name		S	(1)	(1)	(1)	(1)	(1)	(1)
Application for Sales Tax Permit	Reg 1	S	(1)	(1)	(1)	(1)	(1)	(1)
Certificate of Incorporation/Appointment of Agent		S	N	N	Y	Y	Y	Y
Organization and First Biennial Report		S	N	N	Y	Y	Y	Y
Franchise Tax		S	N	N	Y	Y	Y	Y
Business License		S/L	(1)	(1)	(1)	(1)	(1)	(1)

Key to abbreviations:
Y = Form required
N = Form not required
S = State
F = Federal
L = Local
1 = If applicable for type of business

Appendix D - Important business reporting dates - Proprietors

Note: The table below assumes that the owner's tax year ends on December 31. The income tax forms have different due dates for owners who use a different accounting year. It also assumes the owner has minimal sales tax and withholding tax to send. If these taxes are greater the owner must make more frequent deposits.

Due Date	Form No	Sent to	Explanation
Jan 15	8109	Bank	Withholding (W/H) & FICA
Jan 15	1040ES	IRS	Personal Estimated Tax
Jan 15	CT1040ES	CT DRS	Personal Estimated Tax
Jan 31	941	IRS	W/H & FICA
Jan 31	8109	Bank	Federal Unemployment
Jan 31	940	IRS	Federal Unemployment
Jan 31	W-2	Employees	Wage Withholding
Jan 31	UC-2	CT Dept of Labor	State Unemployment
Jan 31	OS114-T	CT DRS	Sales Tax
Jan 31	1099	Recipient	Information Return
Feb 15	8109	Bank	W/H & FICA
Feb 28	W-3, W-2	Social Security Admin.	Wages
Feb 28	1096, 1099	IRS	Information returns
Mar 15	8109	Bank	W/H & FICA
Apr 15	8109	Bank	W/H & FICA
Apr 15	1040	IRS	Personal Income Tax
Apr 15	CT 1040	CT DRS	CT Personal Income Tax
Apr 15	1040ES	IRS	Personal Estimate (Next Yr)
Apr 15	CT1040ES	CT DRS	Personal Estimate (Next Yr)
Apr 15	8109	Bank	Federal Unemployment
Apr 30	941	IRS	W/H & FICA
Apr 30	UC-2	CT Dept of Labor	State Unemployment
Apr 30	OS114-T	CT DRS	Sales Tax
May 15	8109	Bank	W/H & FICA
Jun 15	8109	Bank	W/H & FICA
Jun 15	1040ES	IRS	Personal Estimated Tax
Jun 15	CT1040ES	CT DRS	Personal Estimated Tax
Jul 15	8109	Bank	W/H & FICA
Jul 31	941	IRS	W/H & FICA
Jul 31	UC-2	CT Dept of Labor	State Unemployment
Jul 31	OS114-T	CT DRS	Sales Tax
Jul 31	5500	IRS	Pension Plan Return
Aug 15	8109	Bank	W/H & FICA
Sep 15	8109	Bank	W/H & FICA
Sep 15	1040ES	IRS	Personal Estimated Tax
Sep 15	CT1040ES	CT DRS	Personal Estimated Tax
Oct 15	8109	Bank	W/H & FICA
Oct 15	8109	Bank	Federal Unemployment
Oct 31	941	IRS	W/H & FICA
Oct 31	UC-2	CT Dept of Labor	State Unemployment
Oct 31	OS114-T	CT DRS	Sales Tax
Nov 1	Varies	Local town	Property tax return
Nov 15	8109	Bank	W/H & FICA
Dec 15	8109	Bank	W/H & FICA

Appendix E-Important business reporting dates-Partnership & LLCs

Note: The table below assumes that the company's accounting year ends on December 31. The income tax forms have different due dates for companies that use a different accounting year. It also assumes the company has minimal sales tax and withholding tax to send. If these taxes are greater the company must make more frequent deposits. Besides the IRS forms for the partnership, each partner is responsible for personal tax returns and estimated payments.

Due Date	Form No	Sent to	Explanation
Jan 15	8109	Bank	Withholding (W/H) & FICA
Jan 31	941	IRS	W/H & FICA
Jan 31	8109	Bank	Federal Unemployment
Jan 31	940	IRS	Federal Unemployment
Jan 31	W-2	Employees	Wage Withholding
Jan 31	UC-2	CT Dept of Labor	State Unemployment
Jan 31	OS114-T	CT DRS	Sales Tax
Jan 31	1099	Recipient	Information Return
Feb 15	8109	Bank	W/H & FICA
Feb 28	W-3, W-2	Social Security Admin.	Wages
Feb 28	1096, 1099	IRS	Information returns
Mar 15	8109	Bank	W/H & FICA
Apr 15	8109	Bank	W/H & FICA
Apr 15	8109	Bank	Federal Unemployment
Apr 15	1065	IRS	Partnership Return
Apr 15	CT1065	CT DRS	Partnership Return
Apr 30	941	IRS	W/H & FICA
Apr 30	UC-2	CT Dept of Labor	State Unemployment
Apr 30	OS114-T	CT DRS	Sales Tax
May 15	8109	Bank	W/H & FICA
Jun 15	8109	Bank	W/H & FICA
Jul 15	8109	Bank	W/H & FICA
Jul 31	941	IRS	W/H & FICA
Jul 31	UC-2	CT Dept of Labor	State Unemployment
Jul 31	OS114-T	CT DRS	Sales Tax
Jul 31	5500	IRS	Pension Plan Return
Aug 15	8109	Bank	W/H & FICA
Sep 15	8109	Bank	W/H & FICA
Oct 15	8109	Bank	W/H & FICA
Oct 15	8109	Bank	Federal Unemployment
Oct 31	941	IRS	W/H & FICA
Oct 31	UC-2	CT Dept of Labor	State Unemployment
Oct 31	OS114-T	CT DRS	Sales Tax
Nov 1	Varies	Local town	Property tax return
Nov 15	8109	Bank	W/H & FICA
Dec 15	8109	Bank	W/H & FICA

Appendix F - Important business reporting dates - "S" Corporations

Note: The table below assumes that the company's accounting year ends on December 31. The income tax forms have different due dates for companies that use a different accounting year. It also assumes the company has minimal sales tax and withholding tax to send. If these taxes are greater the company must make more frequent deposits.

Due Date	Form No	Sent to	Explanation
Jan 15	8109	Bank	Withholding (W/H) & FICA
Jan 31	941	IRS	W/H & FICA
Jan 31	8109	Bank	Federal Unemployment
Jan 31	940	IRS	Federal Unemployment
Jan 31	W-2	Employees	Wage Withholding
Jan 31	UC-2	CT Dept of Labor	State Unemployment
Jan 31	OS114-T	CT DRS	Sales Tax
Jan 31	1099	Recipient	Information Return
Jan 31	61-10	CT Sec of State	Annual/Biennial Report
Feb 15	8109	Bank	W/H & FICA
Feb 28	W-3, W-2	Social Security Admin.	Wages
Feb 28	1096, 1099	IRS	Information returns
Mar 15	8109	Bank	W/H & FICA
Mar 15	1120S	IRS	Corporate Income Tax
Mar 15	CT1120ES	CT DRS	State Corp Estimated
Apr 1	CT1120S	CT DRS	State Income Tax
Apr 15	8109	Bank	W/H & FICA
Apr 15	8109	Bank	Federal Unemployment
Apr 30	941	IRS	W/H & FICA
Apr 30	UC-2	CT Dept of Labor	State Unemployment
Apr 30	OS114-T	CT DRS	Sales Tax
May 15	8109	Bank	W/H & FICA
Jun 15	8109	Bank	W/H & FICA
Jun 15	CT1120ES	CT DRS	State Corp Estimated
Jul 15	8109	Bank	W/H & FICA
Jul 31	941	IRS	W/H & FICA
Jul 31	UC-2	CT Dept of Labor	State Unemployment
Jul 31	OS114-T	CT DRS	Sales Tax
Jul 31	5500	IRS	Pension Plan Return
Aug 15	8109	Bank	W/H & FICA
Sep 15	8109	Bank	W/H & FICA
Sep 15	CT1120ES	CT DRS	State Corp Estimated
Oct 15	8109	Bank	W/H & FICA
Oct 15	8109	Bank	Federal Unemployment
Oct 31	941	IRS	W/H & FICA
Oct 31	UC-2	CT Dept of Labor	State Unemployment
Oct 31	OS114-T	CT DRS	Sales Tax
Nov 1	Varies	Local town	Property tax return
Nov 15	8109	Bank	W/H & FICA
Dec 15	8109	Bank	W/H & FICA
Dec 15	CT1120ES	CT DRS	State Corp Estimated

Appendix G - Important business reporting dates - "C" Corporations

Note: The table below assumes that the company's accounting year ends on December 31. The income tax forms have different due dates for companies that use a different accounting year. It also assumes the company has minimal sales tax and withholding tax to send. If these taxes are greater the company must make more frequent deposits.

Due Date	Form No	Sent to	Explanation
Jan 15	8109	Bank	Withholding (W/H) & FICA
Jan 31	941	IRS	W/H & FICA
Jan 31	8109	Bank	Federal Unemployment
Jan 31	940	IRS	Federal Unemployment
Jan 31	W-2	Employees	Wage Withholding
Jan 31	UC-2	CT Dept of Labor	State Unemployment
Jan 31	OS114-T	CT DRS	Sales Tax
Jan 31	1099	Recipient	Information Return
Jan 31	61-10	CT Sec of State	Annual/Biennial Report
Feb 15	8109	Bank	W/H & FICA
Feb 28	W-3, W-2	Social Security Admin.	Wages
Feb 28	1096, 1099	IRS	Information returns
Mar 15	8109	Bank	W/H & FICA
Mar 15	1120	IRS	Corporate Income Tax
Mar 15	CT1120ES	CT DRS	State Corp Estimated
Apr 1	CT 1120	CT DRS	State Income Tax
Apr 15	8109	Bank	W/H & FICA
Apr 15	1120W	IRS	Corp Estimate (Next Yr)
Apr 15	8109	Bank	Federal Unemployment
Apr 30	941	IRS	W/H & FICA
Apr 30	UC-2	CT Dept of Labor	State Unemployment
Apr 30	OS114-T	CT DRS	Sales Tax
May 15	8109	Bank	W/H & FICA
Jun 15	8109	Bank	W/H & FICA
Jun 15	CT1120ES	CT DRS	State Corp Estimated
Jun 15	1120W	Bank	Federal Corp Estimated
Jul 15	8109	Bank	W/H & FICA
Jul 31	941	IRS	W/H & FICA
Jul 31	UC-2	CT Dept of Labor	State Unemployment
Jul 31	OS114-T	CT DRS	Sales Tax
Jul 31	5500	IRS	Pension Plan Return
Aug 15	8109	Bank	W/H & FICA
Sep 15	8109	Bank	W/H & FICA
Sep 15	1120W	Bank	Federal Corp Estimated
Sep 15	CT1120ES	CT DRS	State Corp Estimated
Oct 15	8109	Bank	W/H & FICA
Oct 15	8109	Bank	Federal Unemployment
Oct 31	941	IRS	W/H & FICA
Oct 31	UC-2	CT Dept of Labor	State Unemployment
Oct 31	OS114-T	CT DRS	Sales Tax
Nov 1	Varies	Local town	Property tax return
Nov 15	8109	Bank	W/H & FICA
Dec 15	8109	Bank	W/H & FICA
Dec 15	CT1120ES	CT DRS	State Corp Estimated
Dec 15	1120W	Bank	Federal Corp Estimated

Appendix H - Important business reporting dates - Nonprofit

Note: The table below assumes that the company's accounting year ends on December 31. The income tax forms have different due dates for companies that use a different accounting year. It also assumes the company has minimal sales tax and withholding tax to send. If these taxes are greater the company must make more frequent deposits.

Due Date	Form No	Sent to	Explanation
Jan 15	8109	Bank	Withholding (W/H) & FICA
Jan 31	941	IRS	W/H & FICA
Jan 31	8109	Bank	Federal Unemployment
Jan 31	940	IRS	Federal Unemployment
Jan 31	W-2	Employees	Wage Withholding
Jan 31	UC-2	CT Dept of Labor	State Unemployment
Jan 31	OS114-T	CT DRS	Sales Tax
Jan 31	1099	Recipient	Information Return
Jan 31	61-10	CT Sec of State	Annual/Biennial Report
Feb 15	8109	Bank	W/H & FICA
Feb 28	W-3, W-2	Social Security Admin.	Wages
Feb 28	1096, 1099	IRS	Information returns
Mar 15	8109	Bank	W/H & FICA
Apr 15	8109	Bank	W/H & FICA
Apr 15	8109	Bank	Federal Unemployment
Apr 30	941	IRS	W/H & FICA
Apr 30	UC-2	CT Dept of Labor	State Unemployment
Apr 30	OS114-T	CT DRS	Sales Tax
May 15	8109	Bank	W/H & FICA
May 15	990	IRS	Non-profit Organization Return
Jun 15	8109	Bank	W/H & FICA
Jul 15	8109	Bank	W/H & FICA
Jul 31	941	IRS	W/H & FICA
Jul 31	UC-2	CT Dept of Labor	State Unemployment
Jul 31	OS114-T	CT DRS	Sales Tax
Jul 31	5500	IRS	Pension Plan Return
Aug 15	8109	Bank	W/H & FICA
Sep 15	8109	Bank	W/H & FICA
Oct 15	8109	Bank	W/H & FICA
Oct 15	8109	Bank	Federal Unemployment
Oct 31	941	IRS	W/H & FICA
Oct 31	UC-2	CT Dept of Labor	State Unemployment
Oct 31	OS114-T	CT DRS	Sales Tax
Nov 1	Varies	Local town	Property tax return
Nov 15	8109	Bank	W/H & FICA
Dec 15	8109	Bank	W/H & FICA

Appendix I - Where to find government forms for businesses

STATE TAXES

Department of Revenue Services
92 Farmington Avenue
Hartford, CT 06105
566-8520
(800) 321-7829

FEDERAL TAXES

Internal Revenue Service
135 High Street
Hartford, CT 06103
Walk-in service only: no forms available by phone

Internal Revenue Service
Telephone forms order service
(800) 829-3676

STATE AND FEDERAL TAXES

United States Postal Service - Most USPS offices carry IRS and Connecticut forms as a customer service. However, the selection is limited to the most popular forms for individual taxpayers.

Public libraries - Town libraries are also a source of the popular IRS and Connecticut forms. The State library, college libraries and some larger local libraries also subscribe to reproducible forms services.

Appendix J - Sources of taxpayer assistance by mail or telephone

STATE TAXES   Department of Revenue Services
92 Farmington Avenue
Hartford, CT 06105
(203) 566-8520
(800) 321-7829

FEDERAL TAXES   Internal Revenue Service
135 High Street
Hartford, CT 06103
(203) 240-3349
(800) 829-1040

Appendix K - Checklist of cash required to start up a business

	Amount You need
Start-up expense item	
Equipment and other permanent assets:	
Office furnishings	_____
Vehicles	
Machinery	_____
Computers	_____
Office remodeling	_____
Telephone system	_____
Deposits:	
Telephone	_____
Electric	_____
Rent	_____
Insurance	_____
Office supplies	_____
Merchandise inventory	_____
Franchise fees and similar charges	_____
Operating expenses for six to twelve months:	
Advertising	_____
Auto and Truck	_____
Fringe benefits	_____
Communications	_____
Entertainment	_____
Insurance	_____
Interest	_____
Payroll	_____
Postage	_____
Professional fees	_____
Rent	_____
Repairs	_____
Supplies	_____
Taxes	_____
Travel	_____
Utilities	_____
Personal living expenses for six to twelve months:	
Rent or mortgage	_____
Food and clothing	_____
Education	_____
Medical expenses	_____
"Cushion" of five to ten percent of above	_____
Total needed	
	_____

Appendix L - Checklist of cash available to start up a business

Start-up cash available	Amount You have
Savings	_____
Loans:	
Home equity loan	_____
Business loan from bank	_____
Small Business Administration loan	_____
Connecticut Development Authority loan	_____
Friends	_____
Relatives	_____
Venture capital	_____
Suppliers	_____
Customers	_____
Total available	_____

Appendix M - Payroll services in Connecticut

Automatic Data Processing
1047 Main Street
East Hartford, CT
(203) 528-9001

Data Management, Inc.
537 New Britain Avenue
PO Box 789
Farmington, CT 06034

Interpay, Inc.
675 West Johnson Avenue
Cheshire, CT 06410
(203) 272-0361

Paychex Payroll Services
175 Capitol Boulevard, Suite 201
Rocky Hill, CT 06067
(203) 257-0677

Payroll 1
Cromwell West Office Park
160 West Street, Building 1
Cromwell, CT 06416
(203) 635-2444

Appendix N - One-write bookkeeping services in Connecticut

Accu-rite Systems Specialists
12 Chapel Street
P. O. Box 4310
Wallingford, CT
(203) 265-5686

Data Management, Inc.
537 New Britain Avenue
PO Box 789
Farmington, CT 06034

McBee One-Write Bookkeeping
45 South Main Street
West Hartford, CT
(203) 232-6444

Safeguard Business Systems
3460 Main Street
Hartford, CT
(203) 247-2086

Other bookkeeping systems:

Dome Publishing, sold in most stationery stores.

Appendix O - Selected publications for small businesses

The ABC's of Borrowing. Fort Worth, TX: U.S. Small Business Administration, Office of Business Development, 1986.

Americans with Disabilities Act. Washington DC: U.S. Department of Justice, Civil Rights Division, 1990.

The Business Plan. Rocky Hill, CT: Small Business Services, Connecticut Department of Economic Development.

Business Plan for Small Construction Firms. Fort Worth, TX: U.S. Small Business Administration, Office of Business Development, 1986.

Business Planning Guide: Creating a Plan for Success in Your Own Business. Fifth edition, revised and expanded. Dover, NH: Upstart Publishing, Inc., 1989.

Checklist for Going Into Business. Fort Worth, TX: U.S. Small Business Administration, Office of Business Development.

Connecticut Sourcebook. Deloitte & Touche, and Shipman & Goodman. Edition III. Privately printed, 1989.

The Business Plan for Homebased Business. Eliason, Carol. Fort Worth, TX: U.S. Small Business Administration, Office of Business Development, 1987.

Monthly Cash Flow Projection. Connecticut Small Business Development Center, 1988.

Business Plan for Small Service Firms. Office of Management Assistance, U.S. Small Business Administration, Fort Worth, TX: U.S. Small Business Administration, Office of Business Development.

Operating Plan Forecast (Profit and Loss Projection). Connecticut Small Business Development Center, 1988.

Business Planning Worksheets. Osgood, William R., Durham, NH: developed by Office of Small Business Programs, University of New Hampshire, sponsored by Connecticut Small Business Development Center, University of Connecticut, 1984.

Starting a Home-Based Business. Rice, Frederick H., Fourth ed. Manhattan, KS: Kansas State University, 1990.

Thinking About Going Into Business? Roussel, F.J. and Epplin, Rose. Fort Worth, TX: U.S. Small Business Administration, Office of Business Development, 1988.

Small Business Directory: Publications and Videotapes for Starting and Managing a Successful Small Business. U.S. Small Business Administration, Office of Business Development, Fort Worth, TX.

A Pricing Checklist for Small Retailers. Walker, Bruce J.,Fort Worth, TX: U.S. Small Business Administration, Office of Business Development.

Basic Budgets for Profit Planning. Woelfel, Charles J., Fort Worth, TX: U.S. Small Business Administration, Office of Business Development, 1988.

On Your Own: A Woman's Guide to Building a Business. Zukerman, Laurie B., Dover, NH: Upstart Publishing Company, Inc., 1990.

Part 1 - Departments that offer assistance to small businesses and also supervise licensing of professions and trades.

ACCOUNTING

State Board of Accountancy
30 Trinity Street
Hartford, CT 06106
(203) 566-7835

AGRICULTURE

Department of Agriculture
State Office Building
Hartford, CT 06106
(203) 566-5970

BANKING

Department of Banking
44 Capitol Avenue
Hartford, CT 06106
(203) 566-4560

CONSUMER PROTECTION

Department of Consumer Protection
State Office Building
Hartford, CT 06106

Architectural Registration Board, (203) 566-3290
Division of Athletics, (203) 566-3843
Division of Bedding and Product Safety, (203) 566-2816
Division of Drug Control, (203) 566-4490
State Board of Engineers and Land Surveyors, (203) 566-3386
Food Division, (203) 566-3388
Division of Fraud, (203) 566-4807
State Board of Occupational Licensing, (203) 566-3290
Pharmacy Commission, (203) 566-3917
Real Estate Commission, (203) 566-5130
Department of Forestry & Horticulture, Box 1106, New Haven, CT 06504, (203) 789-7252
Public Charities Unit, 30 Trinity Street, Hartford, CT 06106, (203) 566-5836
TV and Radio Examiners, (203) 566-5547
Division of Weights and Measures, (203) 566-4778, (203) 566-5230

EDUCATION

Department of Education
79 Elm Street
Hartford, CT 06106-5127
(203) 566-5497

ENVIRONMENTAL PROTECTION

Department of Environmental Protection
79 Elm Street
Hartford, CT 06106-5127
(203) 566-3900

HEALTH SERVICES

Department of Health Services
150 Washington Street
Hartford, CT 06106-5127
(203) 566-4800

INSURANCE

Department of Insurance
State Office Building
Hartford, CT 06103
(203) 566-3900

LABOR

Department of Labor
200 Folly Brook Blvd.
Wethersfield, CT 06109
(203) 566-5160

LIQUOR CONTROL

Department of Liquor Control
State Office Building
Hartford, CT 06106
(203) 566-5926

MENTAL RETARDATION

Department of Mental Retardation
98 Pitkin Street
East Hartford, CT 06108
(203) 528-7141

MOTOR VEHICLES   Department of Motor Vehicles
60 State Street
Wethersfield, CT 06109
(203) 566-4712

PUBLIC SAFETY   Division of Fire, Emergency and Building Services
P.O. Box 2794
Middletown, CT 06457-9294
(203) 238-6623

TRANSPORTATION   Department of Transportation
2800 Berlin Turnpike
Newington, CT 06111
(203) 594-2000

Part 2 - Departments and organizations that offer financing and general management assistance.

ACCOUNTING SERVICES   Community Accounting Aid & Services, Inc.
1800 Asylum Avenue, 4th Floor
West Hartford, CT 06117
(203) 241-4984

BUSINESS COUNSELING   Connecticut Small Business Development Center. For information about closest office, contact:

     University of Connecticut
School of Business Administration
368 Fairfield Road, Box U-41
Storrs, CT 06268
(203) 486-4135

     Business Outreach Centers. For service office information, contact:

     Connecticut Economic Resource Center
1-800-392-2122

     Set-aside Program
(For minority vendors)
(203) 258-4373

     Hartford Economic Development Corporation
15 Lewis Street
Hartford, CT 06103
(203) 527-1301

FINANCING SERVICES   Connecticut Development Authority
845 Brook Street
Rocky Hill, CT 06067
(203) 258-7800

     U.S. Small Business Administration
330 Main Street
Hartford, CT 06106
(203) 240-4700

     Connecticut Innovations, Inc.
845 Brook Street
Rocky Hill, CT 06067
(203) 258-4305

     Community Economic Development Fund
(203) 332-7600

CORPORATION
REGISTRATION   Secretary of the State
UCC Division
30 Trinity Street
Hartford, CT 06106
(203) 566-3216

ONE STOP LICENSING   Connecticut Department of Economic Development
865 Brook Street
Rocky Hill, CT 06067
(203) 258-4275

Appendix Q - Federal resources for small businesses

AGRICULTURE

Department of Agriculture
Office of Small and Disadvantaged Business Utilization
Washington, D.C. 20250
(202) 447-7117

COMMERCE

Department of Commerce
Office of Business Liaison
Washington, D.C. 20230
(202) 377-3160

Department of Commerce
Bureau of the Census
Washington, D.C. 20230
(202) 763-4040

DEFENSE

Department of Defense
Director of Small and Disadvantaged Business Utilization
The Pentagon
Washington, D.C. 20301
(202) 697-9387

EDUCATION

Department of Education
Office of Small and Disadvantaged Business Utilization
400 Maryland Avenue SW
Washington, D.C. 20202
(202) 245-3192

ENERGY

Department of Energy
Office of Small and Disadvantaged Business Utilization
Washington, D.C. 20585
(202) 252-8201

ENVIRONMENTAL
PROTECTION

Environmental Protection Agency
Small Business Ombudsman
401 M Street SW
Washington, D.C. 20460
(800) 368-5888

GENERAL SERVICES

General Services Administration
450 Main Street
Hartford, CT 06103
(203) 240-3540

HOUSING

Department of Housing and Urban Development
Office of Small and Disadvantaged Business Utilization
Washington, D.C. 20410
(202) 755-6420

IRS

Internal Revenue Service
135 High Street
Hartford, CT 06103
(203) 240-3349

LABOR

Department of Labor
Office of Small and Disadvantaged Business Utilization
200 Constitution Avenue NW
Washington, D.C. 20210
(202) 523-9148

MINORITY BUSINESS

Minority Business Development Agency
26 Federal Plaza
New York, NY 10278
(212) 264-3262

NATIVE AMERICANS

Department of the Interior, Bureau of Indian Affairs
Small Business Procurement Program
Washington, D.C. 20240
(202) 343-5125

SBA

Small Business Administration
330 Main Street
Hartford, CT 06103
(203) 240-4700

Small Business Administration
Office of Advocacy
Imperial Building, 1441 L Street NW
Washington, D.C. 20416
(202) 653-6808

SOCIAL SECURITY

Social Security Administration
450 Main Street
Hartford, CT 06103
(203) 240-3180

Appendix R - Tax rate and deduction table

Note: To make the book more useful, the authors *purposely* did not list specific tax rates in their material. This is because the rates change often. The tax rates at date of publication are listed below.

Connecticut sales tax

Sales tax on most sales	6.00%
Sales tax on repair parts for manufacturing	4.40%

Connecticut corporation income tax

January 1 to December 31, 1993	11.50%
January 1 to December 31, 1994	11.50%
January 1 to December 31, 1995	11.25%
January 1 to December 31, 1996	11.00%
January 1 to December 31, 1997	10.50%
January 1 to December 31, 1998 and after	10.00%

Federal corporation income tax ("C" corporations)

Maximum rate	35.00%

Connecticut personal income tax

Maximum rate	4.50%

Federal personal income tax

Maximum rate	39.60%

Federal tax deduction limits

Daily deduction for travel expenses	$26.00
Standard mileage rate for business use of a car for 1993	28.5¢

Self employment tax

1993	$0 to $57,600	15.30%
	$57,600 to 135,000	2.90%
1994	$0 to $60,600	15.30%
	over $60,600	2.90%

Social Security tax and medicare

1993	$0 to $57,600	7.65%
	$57,600 to 135,000	1.45%
1994	$0 to $60,600	7.65%
	over $60,600	1.45%

Federal minimum wage

Hourly rate as of January 1, 1994	$4.25

State minimum wage

Hourly rate as of January 1, 1994	$4.27

Appendix S - Records retention guide

One Year

Cash Reports
Department Forecasts
Inventory Tags-Tickets

Packing Slips
Production Orders, Reports
Requisitions
Returned Goods Notices

Two Years

Audit Reports-Internal
Demurrage Notices
Departmental Reports
Express Receipts
Parcel Post Receipts
Payroll Receipts
Purchase Price Records
Purchase Quotations

Sales Orders
Shipping Orders
Standards, Efficiency Records
Stores Records

Three Years

Bills of Lading

General Correspondence

Four Years

Time Cards

Six Years

Accounts Payable Records
Accounts Receivable Records
Bank Statements
Canceled Checks, Stubs
Cash Slips
Claims, Claims Correspondence
Customer Orders
Deposit Slips
Diversion Notices
Draft Registers
Employee Earnings Ledger
Inventory Records

Medical Records
Payroll Data
Purchase Orders
Receiving Slips
Shop, Work Orders-Capital
  Accounts
Termination of Employment
  Records
Vendor's Debits and Credits
Vendor's Invoices
Withholding Statements

Permanent

Accounts Payable Ledgers
Accounts Receivable Ledgers
Appropriations-Capital Accounts
Audits
Blueprints, Product Records
Capital Stock Books
Cash Books, Cash Registers
Cost, Inventory, Production
  Summaries
Employee Record Cards

Financial Statements
General Ledger, Journal
Government Reports
Group Insurance Records
Corporation Meeting Minute
  Books
Notes Payable, Receivable Regis-
  ters
Property Records
Tax Returns-Corporate
Voucher Registers

Appendix T - IRS tax information publications

Note: The Internal Revenue Service publishes hundreds of information publications, covering most major tax topics. Each one summarizes, in one place, all the regulations about a topic. This is a list of publications that would be helpful to small companies.

Publication	Number
Your rights as a taxpayer	1
Travel, entertainment and gift expenses	9
Tax withholding and estimated tax	13
Employer's Tax Guide (Circular E)	15
Business reporting	325
Fuel tax credits and refunds	387
Social Security for members of the clergy and religious workers	517
Charitable contributions	526
Reporting income from tips	531
Self-employment tax	533
Depreciation	534
Business expenses	535
Net operating losses	536
Tax information on partnerships	541
Tax information on corporations	542
Sales and other dispositions of assets	544
Interest expense	545
Basis of assets	551
Determining the value of donated property	561
Tax exempt status for your organization	557
Retirement plans for the self-employed	560
Taxpayers starting a business	583
Business use of your home	587
Tax information on S corporations	589
Tax on unrelated business income of exempt organizations	598
Index to subject matter in IRS publications	910
Tax information for direct sellers	911
Business use of a car	917

Appendix U - Example of a chart of accounts

Account Number	Description
101	Cash
109	Note Receivable
110	Accounts Receivable
115	Inventory
150	Fixed Assets
151	Accumulated Depreciation
160	Organization Costs
161	Accumulated Amortization
201	Accounts Payable
214	Accrued State Income Tax
215	Accrued Federal Income Tax
251	Loans from Shareholders
295	Common Stock
298	Retained Earnings
301	Net Sales
401	Product Cost
403	Storage
405	Freight
409	Commissions
411	Printing
413	Ad Space
415	Fulfillment
417	Art & Design
419	Meals & Entertainment
421	Travel
423	Office Expense
425	Utilities
427	Professional Fees
429	Depreciation
430	Amortization
431	Bad Debt
433	Rent
435	Miscellaneous
498	State Income Tax
499	Federal Income Tax

Appendix V - Balance sheet worksheet

_____

Company name

_____

Date

Assets

Current assets
    Cash $ _____
    Accounts receivable   _____
    Inventory   _____
        Total current assets   _____

Property & equipment
    Equipment   _____
    Vehicles   _____
    Furniture   _____
    Total property and equipment   _____

    Less accumulated depreciation   _____
        Net property and equipment   _____

Total assets $ _____

Liabilities and Shareholders' Equity

Current liabilities
    Accounts payable $ _____
    Notes payable, current   _____
    Accrued expenses & taxes   _____
        Total current liabilities   _____

Other liabilities
    Notes payable, due after one year   _____

Shareholders equity
    Common stock   _____
    Retained earnings   _____
        Total shareholders' equity   _____

Total liabilities & shareholders' equity $ _____

Appendix W - Income statement worksheet

_____
Company name

_____
Date

Sales $_____

Cost of goods sold
    Materials   _____
    Subcontract   _____
    Direct labor   _____

                                                       _____

Gross profit   _____

Operating expenses
    Salaries   _____
    Rent and utilities   _____
    Administrative   _____
    Marketing   _____
    _____   _____

    Total operating expenses   _____

Net income before taxes   _____

Federal income tax   _____
State income tax   _____

Total income tax   _____

Net income after taxes $_____

Appendix X - Business purchase checklist - Page 1

Note: This checklist should be used as a starting point to supplement a buyer's judgement and initiative. It was drawn from several sources including the author's experience and is somewhat generic. Don't use it without customizing it for the circumstances.

1.   General considerations

    1.   Description of the company
        Company history
        What is for sale - Entire company, part of it, partial interest?
        Why is company for sale?
        Evaluation of industry and growth potential
        Status of company within its industry
        Capital structure

    2.   Markets and competitors
        Markets served
        Potential new markets
        Growing, mature or declining market?
        Proposed new products
        Principal competitors
        Effects of economic developments, tax changes or legislation

    3.   Capital requirements

    4.   Location and facilities

    5.   Evaluation of:
            Management
            Production
            Work force

    6.   Sales and marketing - Analysis of current and potential
        Sales promotion methods
        Relationship between company and its customers
        Sales:
            By product
            By major customer
            By market
        Particulars of any major open contracts
        Any fixed price or long-term contracts?
        Any controls on selling prices by government, etc.?

2. **Legal considerations**

    1.   Corporate, statutory and regulatory documents

    2.   Contractual obligations, other than management or labor
            Loan agreements
            Government and/or long-term contracts
            Leases
            Licenses
            Franchises
            Mortgages
            Insurance policies
            Are contracts assignable?

    3.   Management/labor obligations

    4.   Pension, profit sharing, and other employee benefits

    5.   Property titles and liens
            Intangible personal property (patents, trademarks, etc.)
            Existing liens
            Pending legislation

3. **Accounting considerations**

    1.   Accounting policies - Compliance with accounting standards

    2.   Financial statements
            Balance sheet items
            Assets
                 Accounts receivable and bad debt reserve
                 Inventory
                      Inventory turnover, basis of valuation
                      Methods for slow-moving and obsolete inventory
                 Building and equipment
                      Real and personal property taxes
                      Relation of cost to appraisal value and market value
                      Depreciation rates
                      Replacement policy
                 Intangible assets
                      Patents, trademarks, designs
                      Goodwill
                 Investments

Liabilities
    Bank and other Debt
        Amounts
        Dates of repayment
        Interest rates
        Security
    Availability of further financing
    Leasing agreements
    Guarantees
    Contingent liabilities
    Discounted bills
    Litigation pending
    Arrangements for company cars
Income statement
    Gross profit ratio
    Comparison with other companies
    Operating profit ratio
    Do expenses include personal items of owners?
    Nonrecurring income and expenses
    Analysis of executive salaries and bonuses
    Explanation of fluctuations in income or expense
    Sales
        Trends
        Back orders
    Cost of sales and expenses
        Percentage margin on sales
        Method of spreading profit on long term contracts
        Interest and costs of borrowing
        General and administrative expenses
Sources and uses of cash
Adequacy of working capital
Relationship with bankers
Other considerations
    Insured values
    Any material purchase commitments?
    Deferred pension plan costs, if any?
    Nonqualified pension agreements - Extent of liability
    Agreements, written or unwritten, regarding expenses
Taxes
    Adequacy of income tax liability
    Possible additional taxes for prior years
    Any years closed by IRS?
    Any audits in progress with IRS or state?
    Details of loss carry forwards

ORDER FORM

for

STARTING A SMALL BUSINESS IN CONNECTICUT

Fill out and return to:

Community Accounting Aid & Services, Inc.
1800 Asylum Avenue, 4th Floor
West Hartford, CT
06117

Please send me a copy of the new Starting a Small Business in Connecticut. Enclosed is a check for $28.95 made payable to CAAS.

(The price equals $24.95 plus sales tax of $1.50 and shipping/handling of $2.50).

Name:_____

Address:_____

City:_____ State:_____ Zip:_____

Daytime Telephone:_____

If you would like to order more than one copy, please call the CAAS office at 241-4984 to obtain correct pricing.

- -

ORDER FORM

for

STARTING A SMALL BUSINESS IN CONNECTICUT

Fill out and return to:

Community Accounting Aid & Services, Inc.
1800 Asylum Avenue, 4th Floor
West Hartford, CT
06117

Please send me a copy of the new Starting a Small Business in Connecticut. Enclosed is a check for $28.95 made payable to CAAS.

(The price equals $24.95 plus sales tax of $1.50 and shipping/handling of $2.50).

Name:_____

Address:_____

City:_____ State:_____ Zip:_____

Daytime Telephone:_____

If you would like to order more than one copy, please call the CAAS office at 241-4984 to obtain correct pricing.